FOR THE RECORD

MY 1,000 FAVORITE ALBUMS

1957-2017

BRYAN O'CONNOR

Printed in the United States of America

ISBN: 978-0-578-46822-8

Library of Congress Control Number: 2019902442

Published by:
Bryan O'Connor
Cumberland Foreside
Maine 04110

Book design by Tamara Jones

FOR THE RECORD

● ● ● ● ●

MY 1,000 FAVORITE ALBUMS

1957-2017

BRYAN O'CONNOR

TABLE OF CONTENTS

● ● ● ● ●

INTRODUCTION:
HOW DID WE GET HERE?

● ● ● ● ●

Thank you for visiting the Amateur Music ~~Criticism~~ Obsessive Consumption and Comparative Analysis section of your local bookstore. I'm sure it was crowded.

In the pages ahead, you'll read about my 1,000 favorite albums released between 1957 and 2017. While ranking music may seem like a hollow pursuit, there's a good chance I'm not the only person you know who consumes music this way. Countless publications periodically release lists of their top albums of the year or decade. At besteveralbums.com, a community of thousands of amateur critics has collectively published almost 65,000 lists of their favorite albums. Similar communities exist at rateyourmusic.com, ranker.com, and elsewhere.

Art is entertainment, and for many of us, the best way to relate to art is to compare it to other art.

As with all arts, any assessment of the quality of music is subjective. For those of us whose brains prefer data to anecdote, quantity to quality, compiling listening experiences and rating and ranking music is a way to find data in the subjective. There's no verifiable truth to my assessment that Radiohead released six albums better than U2's second-best. Once that assessment is recorded as data, though, it can help me reach easy conclusions like "I like Radiohead's music far more than

U2's" and more interesting conclusions like "in my estimation, Radiohead's collective output in the 2000's tops anyone else's, and they were fourth in the 1990s too."

If you love music and you appreciate the search for objectivity in the subjective world, I think this list and the accompanying essays will be of interest to you. If you don't care about data and are just here for the music, here are 1,000 opinions with which for you to nod in approval or curl your lip in disgust.

With streaming services available, our options as to what music to listen to are endless. Mostly for my own benefit, my listening experience, particularly over the past several years, is very well documented. I hope sharing it in this format leads you to a few albums that enrich your life in some small way.

WHY 1,000 ALBUMS?

A thousand grains of sand won't fill up your hand. A thousand hits won't get a baseball player into the Hall of Fame. But a thousand albums take two months to slog through if all you do for those two months is sleep and listen to music. Why would anyone take on a project of this size with little obvious financial or social benefit?

I'll admit that a major reason I landed on 1,000 is because it's a round number. If we used a base-8 number system instead of base-10, I probably would have stopped at 512 albums just to get to that round number. But it's more than that.

In high school, two friends of mine put together a collective list of the 69 best albums they'd ever heard. I mostly listened to the same two Smashing Pumpkins albums and my dad's Creedence Clearwater Revival hits collection at the time, so I had nothing to add to their project, but after looking at their list, I started consuming music differently.

Before seeing my friends' top 69, I grew my CD* collection by buying everything my four or five favorite bands put out, suffering the new Bush album because I liked the first one.** I liked what I liked and couldn't afford to spend $14 per disc exploring genres I might not care for. Thinking about music criticism by comparison helped me parse collections by my favorite bands while expanding into other genres with money I might have wasted by trying to build my collection of Oasis records.

I forayed into classic rock, diving in headfirst with guidance from allmusic.com and Rolling Stone magazine. Years later, I took a stab at jazz, just scraping the surface based on recommendations from my friend Mark. I eventually embraced hip-hop, letting friends and critics tell me which Roots and Jay-Z albums were essential and which I could live without. By the time I discovered Pandora and Grooveshark and Spotify and had the freedom to explore electronica, dubstep, and, somewhat reluctantly, even country, at little-to-no-cost, I had Pitchfork and NME by my side, telling me where my efforts would be rewarded and which landmines to avoid.

I think the first albums list I ever made was a top ten restricted to the still-active 1990s, with Pearl Jam's "Ten" coming out on top. In college, as I got more comfortable with Microsoft Excel, I stopped making new lists every few months and maintained an active list I could easily update with a new favorite. I remember dark days of including albums I'd never heard based on the strength of three or four radio singles I really liked. Hey, I never claimed to be a professional.

---

* *CD stands for compact disc, a round piece of plastic on which digital information is stored, and from which the information can be read using reflected laser light. They once held music.*

** *I no longer like the first Bush album. You might. No judgment here.*

It wasn't until 2009, when my daughter was born, that I first got heavily into new music and started making year-end lists. My cousin Ryan and my friend Pat kept me stocked with burned CDs and Grooveshark links to new music and bands like Grizzly Bear and Dirty Projectors had me wondering why I'd lived in the past for so long when the present was as strong as ever.

When I first bought a Spotify premium account a few years later, I could listen to just about anything, anywhere, at any time, and I've made sure to get the most out of my $10 per month. During the second half of every year, I make a list of my fifty favorite new releases, and in the first half, I tend to bury myself in a project, like scouring the complete canon of a few artists I like or traveling back through time and building a top-25 list for every year from the '70s through the '90s. When I extended this last project into the 21st century, I heard the album that convinced me it was worth growing the list to a thousand: "The Grey Album", by Danger Mouse.

Jay-Z's "Black Album" may be his most lyrically-rich offering. Billed as a swan song, it documents with refreshing intimacy the rapper's life to-date and, rather than dissing the competition, he uses his throne to thank those who contributed to his success and wish the best to those in his wake. All that said, it's intentionally sparse in production, letting the raps do the talking. The Beatles' "White Album" is one of rock's first overambitious, throw-it-all-in-the-blender statements: two hours of rock, country, blues, show tunes, and satanic verses that broadened the palette of rock music to come.

Producer Danger Mouse saw an opportunity to bridge the worlds of two of music's legends from different sides of the tracks (and the Atlantic) and brilliantly forged black and white into a masterpiece of grey. This is no Dark-Side-meets-Wizard-of-Oz, play-one-over-the-other mashup. Danger Mouse lets

Jay-Z drive, mixing up the tracklist but essentially laying his entire vocal track over a fine-tuned amalgamation of White Album backing tracks, improving upon the original production and creating an album I couldn't leave off my list. Tracks like "Encore" and "Lucifer 9" that celebrate the Beatles' darker side distract a bit from Jay-Z's storytelling, keeping this album from the upper echelon, but if an album this great is my thousandth favorite, it's worth listing a thousand.

WHY 1957-2017?

Well, I'm writing this in 2018, so it doesn't make sense to include albums not released yet. As for the 1957 cutoff, it's a clean 60 years*.

More importantly, I can't listen to all the music that was ever recorded, so I have to set some limits, right? Music has been played forever and recorded since the late 1870s. There are centuries of classical music I haven't explored. There are archives of American roots music I haven't studied. What I have explored, quite deeply, are rock and roll, which was, by most accounts, born in the fifties; jazz, which peaked in the late fifties, country, which came of age in the fifties, and several genres and subgenres that evolved and thrived in the past sixty years.

The album as we've come to know it was invented in the late 1940s or early 1950s, depending on one's source. Louis Armstrong and Ella Fitzgerald were making great music in the early fifties and Bill Haley and Elvis Presley broke through in '55 and '56, respectively. It was 1957, though, that gave us the debuts of Chuck Berry, Little Richard, and Johnny Cash, along with peak releases by Coltrane, Monk, and Buddy Holly. This is where we'll start.

---

* *I know, it's 61 when I include both 1957 and 2017, but doesn't it sound cleaner than "1958 to 2017"?*

I also excluded hits compilations, live albums, and short-running EPs, all in the interest of attempting to hear everything that might reasonably make my list without quitting my job and leaving my family.

Without further ado, here are my 1,000 favorite full-length studio albums released between 1957 and 2017, counted down from number 1,000 to number one.

ALBUMS
1000-901

● ● ● ● ●

These first albums skew contemporary, with 47 of 100 released in the 21st century and seven of every ten since 1990. We see names like Bob Dylan, Neil Young, Van Morrison, R.E.M., Sonic Youth, and Beck, all of whom occupy more precious real estate on future pages as well, alongside one-and-dones like Califone, Placebo, Rhye, and Young Marble Giants.

1000. "The Grey Album", Danger Mouse, 2004

999. "Still Bill", Bill Withers, 1972

998. "If I Should Fall From Grace With God", The Pogues, 1988

997. "The Sea and Cake", The Sea and Cake, 1994

996. "The Slow Wonder", AC Newman, 2004

> *AC Newman is one of three members of The New Pornographers, along with Neko Case and Dan Bejar (as Destroyer), to land a solo album on this list.*

995. "Loud City Song", Julia Holter, 2013

994. "Quality Control", Jurassic 5, 2000

993. "Santogold", Santigold, 2008

992. "Souvenirs d'un Autre Monde", Alcest, 2007

991. "Children Running Through", Patty Griffin, 2007

990. "Complicated Game", James McMurtry, 2015

989. "Cold House", Hood, 2001

988. "I Could Live in Hope", Low, 1994

987. "Gentlemen", The Afghan Whigs, 1993

986. "Fumbling Toward Ecstasy", Sarah McLachlan, 1993

985. "Murray Street", Sonic Youth, 2002

984. "Adore Life", Savages, 2016

> *Where Siouxsie and the Banshees meet Sleater-Kinney, you'll find Savages, whose first two albums are both so full of vim and ferocity that I suspect a list of my favorite albums from 1970 to 2030 might include four or five of their records.*

983. "Salad Days", Mac Demarco, 2014

982. "Liars", Liars, 2007

981. "The Wild Hunt", The Tallest Man on Earth, 2010

980. "Dr. Octagonecologyst", Dr. Octagon, 1996

979. "It's Blitz!", The Yeah Yeah Yeahs, 2009

978. "Castaways and Cutouts", The Decemberists, 2002

977. "St. Dominic's Preview", Van Morrison, 1972

976. "Everyday Robots", Damon Albarn, 2014

975. "Q: Are We Not Men? A: We Are Devo", Devo, 1978

974. "Watermelon, Chicken, & Gritz", Nappy Roots, 2002

973. "Fourteen Autumns and Fifteen Winters",
The Twilight Sad, 2007

972. "John Wesley Harding", Bob Dylan, 1968

971. "Showbiz", Muse, 1999

970. "Mutations", Beck, 1998

969. "Parc Avenue", Plants and Animals, 2008

> *"Parc Avenue" is one of four albums on this page by Canadian artists. The others are "Fully Completely", "Tonight's the Night", and "Songs of Love and Hate".*

968. "Garbage", Garbage, 1995

967. "Darklands", The Jesus and Mary Chain, 1987

966. "Without You I'm Nothing", Placebo, 1998

965. "Complete Surrender", Slow Club, 2014

964. "George Best", The Wedding Present, 1987

963. "Blowout Comb", Digable Planets, 1994

962. "Ruins", Grouper, 2014

961. "The Beach Boys Today!", The Beach Boys, 1965

960. "Undun", The Roots, 2011

959. "Black Origami", Jlin, 2017

958. "Over-Nite Sensation", Frank Zappa, 1973

957. "Going Blank Again", Ride, 1992

956. "Blazing Arrow", Blackalicious, 2002

955. "Southernplayalisticadillacmusik", OutKast, 1994

> *There are four more fully-realized OutKast albums to come, but the greatest act in hip-hop history never recorded a bad beat for almost the first decade of their career. "Player's Ball" and "Crumblin' Erb" drip with promise of what was to come.*

954. "Bleach", Nirvana, 1989

953. "Your Arsenal", Morrissey, 1992

952. "Lord Willin'", Clipse, 2002

951. "Mermaid Avenue", Billy Bragg & Wilco, 1998

950. "Oceanic", Isis, 2002

949. "Lie Down in the Light", Bonnie "Prince" Billy, 2008

948. "Los Angeles", Flying Lotus, 2008

947. "Fully Completely", The Tragically Hip, 1992

946. "Neu!", Neu!, 1972

945. "Tonight's the Night", Neil Young, 1975

944. "Songs of Love and Hate", Leonard Cohen, 1971

943. "Damaged", Black Flag, 1981

942. "Return to Cookie Mountain", TV on the Radio, 2006

941. "Joan Armatrading", Joan Armatrading, 1976

940. "Isn't Anything", My Bloody Valentine, 1988

939. "Music from the Unrealized Film Script,
Dusk at Cubist Castle", Olivia Tremor Control, 1996

938. "Clouds", Joni Mitchell, 1969

937. "Rid of Me", PJ Harvey, 1993

936. "Reveal", R.E.M., 2001

935. "Smoke Ring for My Halo", Kurt Vile, 2011

934. "Me Against the World", 2Pac, 1995

933. "Ten Love Songs", Susanne Sundfør, 2015

932. "Woman", Rhye, 2013

931. "The Rising Tide", Sunny Day Real Estate, 2000

930. "Electric Music for the Mind and Body",
Country Joe & the Fish, 1967

929. "Tchamantché", Rokia Traoré, 2008

> *"Tchamantché" is the only album on the list by an artist from Mali. Other countries with exactly one appearance include Argentina, Chile, Denmark, Ethiopia, Haiti, Italy, New Zealand, Senegal, and Uganda.*

928. "Colossal Youth", Young Marble Giants, 1980

927. "St. Elsewhere", Gnarls Barkley, 2006

926. "If You Can Believe Your Eyes and Ears",
The Mamas & the Papas, 1966

925. "IV", Badbadnotgood, 2016

924. "Constant Bop", Bop English, 2015

923. "Band on the Run", Paul McCartney and Wings, 1973

922. "Operation: Doomsday", MF Doom, 1999

921. "Diamond Life", Sade, 1984

920. "Girlfriend", Matthew Sweet, 1991

919. "Cut", The Slits, 1979

918. "Lost in a Dream", The War on Drugs, 2014

917. "Transatlanticism", Death Cab for Cutie, 2003

916. "Licensed to Ill", Beastie Boys, 1986

915. "Quicksand/Cradlesnakes", Califone, 2003

914. "Cerulean Salt", Waxahatchee, 2013

913. "Life After Death", Notorious B.I.G., 1997

What does it mean to be someone's 913th favorite album? In this and a few other cases, it means that, buried within this overlong celebration and lamentation of Biggie's newfound celebrity is enough great music to fill a classic album.

912. "At Mount Zoomer", Wolf Parade, 2008

911. "Epic", Sharon Van Etten, 2010

910. "I Want to See the Bright Lights Tonight", Richard and Linda Thompson, 1974

909. "Sylvan Esso", Sylvan Esso, 2014

908. "Vintage Violence", John Cale, 1970

907. "The Hissing of Summer Lawns", Joni Mitchell, 1975

> *"The Hissing of Summer Lawns" is the second of five albums by Joni Mitchell on the list. Among female solo artists, only PJ Harvey landed as many albums on the list as Joni did.*

906. "Breaking Atoms", Main Source, 1991

905. "Bossanova", Pixies, 1990

904. "Blind Faith", Blind Faith, 1969

903. "First Take", Roberta Flack, 1969

902. "Of the Heart, Of the Soul, and Of the Cross: The Utopian Experience", PM Dawn, 1991

901. "R.A.P. Music", Killer Mike, 2012

BIAS IN THIS LIST

• • • • •

The word favorite implies bias. Every list of personal favorites is influenced by the listmaker's tastes and by the universe of music each of us has sought and heard.

Rolling Stone makes these lists every few years and loads them with music by groups of white men who recorded up to and including the release date of "Nevermind". Q and NME load their top-albums lists with The Smiths, Manic Street Preachers, and everything British. Pitchfork regularly reminds us that music became adequate for human consumption only when David Bowie started working with Brian Eno.

A simple way to ask what biases are present in my list is to ask what kind of music I like. That's always been a tough question to answer. I had an alternative rock phase, a Britpop phase, a long classic-rock phase, and then a decade and a half of listening to everything I can get my hands on... or at least everything someone tells me I should get my hands on. That's where we should start.

You probably have a favorite artist who has released ten albums and I've never listened to one of them. I listened to more than 3,500 albums over the past few years in compiling this list, but I must have missed at least 35,000 decent ones. My primary sources for new music today are besteveralbums.

com, which highlights popular music by compiling top-100 lists submitted by users into a master list, and albumoftheyear.org, which compiles critics' reviews of new albums, converts them to numerical scores, and ranks each year's best albums. Every year, I try to hear at least 100 new albums, including at least the top 50 on each site's list. I tend to keep up with albums-of-the-year or -decade lists from various music publications as well, so if a critical mass of professional critics or fans who consider themselves amateur critics liked it, I've probably heard it.

The product of this approach is a list that skews toward the mainstream- or at least toward the stream in which other music rankers swim. If someone else loved it, I've probably given it a shot and may or may not endorsed the critics' opinions. Those personal favorites in your collection that didn't sell a ton of copies or meet critical praise, though, may have eluded my ears.

As you peruse this list, you'll see more albums by R.E.M. (9), Sleater-Kinney (6), and Beck (6) than you might expect. This is evidence that, once I identify an artist as a favorite, I'm willing to dig deeper into their collection than a summary of critical praise might recommend.

I take diversity seriously, not as much for outward appearances as for my own growth. I'm grateful to Kendrick Lamar's music for sharing a perspective about the black experience in 21st-century America. We all need a dose of Liz Phair now and then to counter the machismo of The Rolling Stones. Willie Nelson offers a glimpse into how they live in parts of the country that don't vote like they do where I live. I try to make the universe of music I let into my life look less like the white, upper-middle-class towns where I've spent most of my years and more like a big city or an effective library.

Despite this effort, the sample of albums recommended to me drives some extreme splits along gender and racial lines.

766 of 1,000 albums are by men or groups fronted by a man, versus just 168 by women, with mixed-gender groups making up the difference. 782 are by white artists, with black artists' 189 contributions making up the next largest racial bloc. I made significant efforts to fight these biases by listening to mostly women and black artists in the weeks before I finalized the list, but old habits die hard and three or four listens to a Nina Simone album, no matter how great, struggle to compete with 100 listens to a Led Zeppelin album I picked up in 1998.

I speak English first and almost exclusively, so of course English-language music dominates my list. While these 1,000 albums come from 26 countries and are sung in well over a dozen languages, 624 were recorded by American artists, 253 more by British artists, and another 51 by Canadians. Among non-English-speaking countries, Germany (nine) and France (seven) lead the way, but much of that music is sung in English or not sung at all. I recognize I'm only scraping the surface of a vast world of music. Look, I tried.

Frankly, when it comes to elements of music that grab my attention, lyrics are far down the list. Vocals are important, and having something to say certainly makes vocals stand out, but give me a band feeding off each other's energy for a long, wordless coda ahead of a soft-spoken protest song or a keenly-worded but passionless love song any day.

If there's a theme that runs across my musical preferences, it might be this: I like music that takes chances without veering too far from pop. I can try to appreciate the wildest moments of Captain Beefheart and mid-sixties Coltrane, but I prefer the eccentric pop of Dr. John and early-seventies Miles. I might dig ear candy like peak Madonna and classic Elvis, but I'd rather hear St. Vincent's take with a little salt sprinkled in.

One might observe that the rock canon occupies an

outsized portion of my list. There's no shortage of records by The Beatles, Led Zeppelin, and the rest of the pioneers we're all taught to revere. These conventional tastes might make much of the list feel bland, but I make an effort to sprinkle in the best of Terry Callier and Department of Eagles to avoid hegemony. Other publications created in the same vein as this one tend to spread ranking and reviewing duties across multiple authors, aiming for mass appeal by aggregating opinions. This tends to promote canon, celebrating the U2 records we've all heard over the Twilight Sad album only one of the book's authors loved.

One danger of celebrating canon is that it tends to skew white and male. Rolling Stone's Top 500 Albums don't include a woman or a band fronted by a woman until Joni Mitchell's "Blue" at #30. I happen to agree that "Blue" is the greatest album ever released by a woman. I also understand that Joni's not for everyone. But if you can't find room in your top 29 for Joni or Aretha or Janis or My Bloody Valentine or Portishead, don't pretend that your list speaks for anyone but yourself. I speak only for myself, but I hope this list appeals to a diverse group of readers and listeners.

If you really need favorites, I like Neko's voice, Stevie's brain, Lennon's heart, Etta's lungs, Andre's style, Mingus's growl, Colin Meloy's flare, Jonny Greenwood's fingers, and Andrew Bird's whistle.

ALBUMS
900-801

* * * * *

The second 100 are similarly modern to the first group, 68 of them having been released since 1990. We get our first glimpse of Miles Davis and a second contribution by R.E.M., each of whom will land nine albums on the list, along with solo albums from Morrissey, Hamilton Leithauser, and Jack White, each of whom will show up later with bands they fronted before going solo. It's also a rare glimpse of The Sonics hobnobbing with Sonic Youth.

900. "Eastern Sounds", Yusef Lateef, 1961

> *A first-time listener of "Eastern Sounds" might not believe that Lateef was born in Chattanooga and grew up in Detroit. The first half of this album competes with anything in the jazz canon.*

899. "Little Girl Blue", Nina Simone, 1957

898. "Run the Jewels 2", Run the Jewels, 2014

897. "Past Life", Lost in the Trees, 2014

896. "De Stijl", The White Stripes, 2000

895. "Lifes Rich Pageant" R.E.M., 1986

894. "Avalon", Roxy Music, 1982

893. "Call Me", Al Green, 1973

892. "Not a Pretty Girl", Ani DiFranco, 1995

891. "Love This Giant", David Byrne & St. Vincent, 2012

> *In addition to "Love This Giant", St. Vincent has two solo albums on this list and appears on Andrew Bird's "Break It Yourself". David Byrne shows up five times with Talking Heads, collaborates once with Brian Eno, and provides vocals on Arcade Fire's "The Suburbs".*

890. "Apocalypse 91... the Enemy Strikes Black", Public Enemy, 1991

889. "Someday My Prince Will Come", Miles Davis, 1961

888. "Immigrés", Youssou N'Dour, 1984

887. "Breaking Kayfabe", Cadence Weapon, 2005

886. "Heartland", Owen Pallett, 2010

885. "Alien Lanes", Guided by Voices, 1995

884. "Kate & Anna McGarricle", Kate & Anna McGarricle, 1976

883. "Like Clockwork", Queens of the Stone Age, 2013

882. "Psychic", Darkside, 2013

881. "The Raw and the Cooked",

Fine Young Cannibals, 1988

880. "Stranded", Roxy Music, 1973

879. "The Stage Names", Okkervil River, 2007

878. "It's Album Time", Todd Terje, 2014

877. "Welcome to Sky Valley", Kyuss, 1994

876. "Aqualung", Jethro Tull, 1971

875. "MCII", Mikal Cronin, 2013

874. "New York Dolls", New York Dolls, 1973

873. "Ships", Danielson, 2006

872. "Piñata", Freddie Gibbs & Madlib, 2014

871. "A Nod's as Good as a Wink... to a Blind Horse",
Faces, 1971

870. "Utopia Defeated", D.D Dumbo, 2016

869. "At Least For Now", Benjamin Clementine, 2015

> *Drawing on classical music as much as rock or pop, Benjamin Clementine's debut seems to exist outside of place and time, though its climax comes on a song named for Clementine's hometown of London.*

868. "Black Hours", Hamilton Leithauser, 2014

867. "Painful", Yo La Tengo, 1993

866. "Plastic Beach", Gorillaz, 2010

865. "Power, Corruption, & Lies", New Order, 1983

864. "Dear Science,", TV On the Radio, 2008

863. "Underachievers Please Try Harder",
Camera Obscura, 2003

862. "Goo", Sonic Youth, 1990

861. "The Downward Spiral", Nine Inch Nails, 1994

860. "Phases and Stages", Willie Nelson, 1974

859. "Here are the Sonics!!!", The Sonics, 1965

858. "Frank", Amy Winehouse, 2003

> *Even at the age of 20 and without the Dap-Kings behind her, Amy Winehouse represented the rare combination of a songwriter capable of pop but willing to break the mold and a singer with a voice from the '50s and a wit for the '00s.*

857. "Let it Die", Feist, 2004

856. "Talking Heads '77", Talking Heads, 1977

855. "Strange Geometry", The Clientele, 2005

854. "Rock Bottom", Robert Wyatt, 1974

853. "Who Will Cut Out Hair When We're Gone?",
The Unicorns, 2003

852. "Naveed", Our Lady Peace, 1994

851. "Human Performance", Parquet Courts, 2016

850. "Metamodern Sounds in Country Music",
Sturgill Simpson, 2014

849. "Weather", Me'shell Ndegeocello, 2011

848. "Our House on the Hill", The Babies, 2012

847. "Ben Folds Five", Ben Folds Five, 1995

> *All three albums from Ben Folds Five's original run made the list, but all are outside the top 600. 88 of the 89 other artists with at least three entries on the list crack the top 500 at least once.*

846. "Too Bright", Perfume Genius, 2014

845. "No Cities to Love", Sleater-Kinney, 2015

844. "The Swimming Hour", Andrew Bird, 2001

843. "Metallica", Metallica, 1991

842. "All Hands on the Bad One", Sleater-Kinney, 2000

841. "The Time Has Come", The Chambers Brothers, 1967

840. "The Unauthorized Biography of Reinhold Messner", Ben Folds Five, 1999

839. "Workbook", Bob Mould, 1989

838. "Mosely Shoals", Ocean Colour Scene

837. "Með Suð Í Eyrum Við Spilum Endalaust", Sigur Rós, 2008

836. "Night Train", The Oscar Peterson Trio, 1962

835. "Head Hunters", Herbie Hancock, 1973

834. "Alright, Still", Lily Allen, 2006

833. "Jazz Samba", Stan Getz & Charlie Byrd, 1962

832. "In the Flat Field", Bauhaus, 1980

831. "Atomizer", Big Black, 1986

830. "Stranger in the Alps", Phoebe Bridgers, 2017

829. "Tinderbox", Siouxsie and the Banshees, 1986

828. "Singing Saw", Kevin Morby, 2016

827. "Holy Fire", Foals, 2013

826. "Bandwagonesque", Teenage Fanclub, 1991

825. "Blunderbuss", Jack White, 2012

824. "Buena Vista Social Club",
Buena Vista Social Club, 1997

823. "No Poison No Paradise", Black Milk, 2013

822. "K", Kula Shaker, 1996

821. "23", Blonde Redhead, 2007

820. "Souvlaki", Slowdive, 1993

819. "Satanic Panic in the Attic", Of Montreal, 2004

818. "Heartbreaker", Ryan Adams, 2000

817. "Viva! La Woman", Cibo Matto, 1996

816. "The Royal Scam", Steely Dan, 1976

815. "The Bright Mississippi", Allen Toussaint, 2009

"The Bright Mississippi" is one of just two jazz albums on the list from the first half of the 21st century. The other is "Insipiration Information 3" by Mulatu Astatke and the Heliocentrics.

814. "My Love is Cool", Wolf Alice, 2015

813. "Z", My Morning Jacket, 2005

812. "Howling Bells", Howling Bells, 2006

811. "Aftermath", The Rolling Stones, 1966

810. "The Slider", T. Rex, 1972

809. "The Sophtware Slump", Grandaddy, 2000

808. "Bend Beyond", Woods, 2012

807. "The Warning", Hot Chip, 2006

806. "When I Said I Wanted to Be Your Dog",
     Jens Lekman, 2004

805. "Till the Sun Turns Black", Ray LaMontagne, 2006

804. "Vs.", Mission of Burma, 1982

803. "Pink", Boris, 2005

"Pink" is the only album on the list recorded by a band that formed in Japan. Cibo Matto's Japanese members met in New York, which is also where Mitski records most of her music. Deerhoof formed in San Francisco.

802. "Introducing the Hard Line According to
     Terence Trent D'Arby", Terence Trent D'Arby, 1987

801. "Sign O' the Times", Prince, 1987

CAN TODAY'S MUSIC COMPETE WITH THE CLASSICS?

• • • • •

It would be reductive to boil music fans down to those who prefer today's music and those who prefer the old stuff, but I think if you asked ten friends which group they're in, the majority would land strongly on one side or the other. A strong argument could be made from either side.

I listed more albums from 1969 (32) and 1970 (28) than any other year, but 2007 (27) and 2014 (27) are next. It was certainly easier to forge new ground and stand out above your peers prior to the late 1960s, when cost and access to recording equipment was a significant barrier to entry for musicians, but modern technology allows more bright minds to make their thoughts public and a more diverse spectrum of ways to express those thoughts today. That would help explain the 1960s accounting for 10 of my top 37 albums, while the 2000s lead all decades with 230 albums in the top 1,000.

There's a clear sampling bias here. In preparing this list, I listened to more than 1,700 albums released between 1997 and 2017 and fewer than 800 albums released between 1957 and 1977. It's not just that there's more music available; it's that scores of publications are writing about music in various genres and promoting their favorites, giving audiences so much more new music. Also, I wasn't alive between '57 and '77, so my "personal favorites" from that era are limited to those promoted by critics and historians.

One factor preventing modern albums from reaching the top tiers of the list is the disappearance of counterculture from the distribution networks that typically promote music. In the sixties, Dylan and Coltrane were making art and The Supremes and Herman's Hermits were dominating the airwaves, but the gap between their music was relatively modest compared to the spectrum of music recorded today. Music made more for the critics than the masses then has since found its way to mainstream classic rock radio.

In the seventies, the introspective singer-songwriter movement tempered some of the prior decade's advances. Early heavy metal and prog rock pick picked up that torch, but by the middle of the decade, bands were so obsessed with flaunting their technical prowess that the pop song was briefly on the endangered species list. Enter punk. The Ramones bashed three chords over and over and covered or mimicked fifties bubblegum pop with the dial turned to eleven. Mainstream radio wasn't ready for it, but fans and critics ate it up and legions of imitators expanded the market for new music. Once limited to the Zappas and Velvet Undergrounds of the world, counterculture was now driving a permanent wedge between the music piped through department store speakers and the music blasted in city clubs and teenage bedrooms.

The eighties brought a further departure between mainstream and underground, as we anointed a King and a Queen of Pop just as hardcore took off. Hair bands shredded like their prog rock ancestors while The Replacements and Hüsker Dü reaped all the critical praise for their refusal to conform to the decade's excesses.

Over the next few decades, record companies making pop

music kept perfecting their formula, seeking singers with sex appeal while willing to fix their voices in post-production. They safely crossed genres with teen- and mom-friendly beats and focus-group-tested collaborations to broaden the appeal of their music. Meanwhile, on another planet, Björk, Radiohead, and their ilk took real chances, challenging the guitar-bass-drums rock formula and verse-chorus-verse structure to find ways to express themselves that expanded on, rather than plucking from, the half-century-old-and-growing rock canon.

Today, with attention spans limited to a gif or a Vine, a career of album sales might be less lucrative than a five-second spot backing an Apple commercial. The amount of music recorded outside the studios committed to making Bruno Mars a wealthier Prince would have been unfathomable forty years ago when punk rockers rebelled against the collective mainstream. Today's artists are chasing their own muses in myriad directions, not reacting to trends in the mainstream.

This dwindling counterculture and diversification of new music is quickly evident when one compares my choices from then and now to popular opinion. All of the ten most popular albums of the sixties at besteveralbums.com are among my 32 favorites from that decade and nine of my top ten from the decade are in that website's top 18. We all know the same music from the sixties.

Of the top ten albums from the 2010s at besteveralbums. com, nine are in my top 50, but the inverse is far from true. My five favorite albums from this decade rank 4th, 477th, 703rd, 3rd, and 33nd, respectively. I like most of the popularly acclaimed new music. I also like a lot of music that hasn't reached as many ears.

One way to compare my tastes for various years, decades, and eras is to assign weighted scores to each album. Giving one point to album 1,000 and 5,000 points to album one and filling in the middle with a simple calculation giving more points for the difference between #3 and #4, for example, than the difference between #803 and #804, I assigned a score to each album and summed each year's points.

Here's that calculation:

$$Rank\ Points = [1,001 - (rank)]^{1.233}$$

To wit:

Mission of Burma's "Vs."
$$[1,001 - 804]^{1.233} = 674.6\ Rank\ Points$$

Boris's "Pink"
$$[1,001-803]^{1.233} = 678.9\ Rank\ Points$$

Album #4 (no spoilers)
$$[1,001-4]^{1.233} = 4,981.9\ Rank\ Points$$

Album #3 (no spolers)
$$[1,001-3]^{1.233} = 4,988.0\ Rank\ Points$$

Here are the top ten years:

1. 1969: 90,745 *Rank Points*
2. 1970: 83,958
3. 1971: 65,564
4. 1967: 65,227
5. 1972: 62,215
6. 1968: 60,376

Guess I'm a sucker for classic rock. But then…

7. 2005: 58,312
8. 2007: 56,490
9. 2000: 55,070
10. 1996: 54,231

1962 takes last place with 6,112 Rank Points spread across just five albums (I only listened to 23 albums from that year). Post-1965, the weakest year is 1981, with 12,782 Rank Points from seven albums (I listened to 50; most of them were bad).

Let's look at the decades:

1. 2000s: 493,981   (230 albums by 180 different artists)
2. 1970s: 427,321   (180 by 114 artists)
3. 1990s: 420,449   (180 by 130 artists)
4. 1960s: 331,855   (124 by 85 artists)
5. 2010s: 272,184   (158 by 136 artists)*
6. 1980s: 242,645   (112 by 84 artists)
7. 1950s: 43,798   (16 by 15 artists)**

There's a lot of new music here. While the Beatles and Bob Dylans of the world load up the '60s with high-ranking albums (9 and 7, respectively), the past two decades are stocked with hundreds of different artists charting one album apiece. Only Radiohead (5) and Kendrick Lamar (4) have more than three albums from the 21st century on the list, while everyone from The Notwist to Boris to Kate Tempest landed one.

One thing I hope to accomplish in sharing this list is to make fellow music nuts aware of great albums that top-forty radio doesn't play and whose praises Rolling Stone doesn't sing. You know about The Rolling Stones and Led Zeppelin, and there's no shortage of either in these pages, but if this book leads you to Serena-Maneesh or Comets on Fire, or even if it just adds one Sleater-Kinney album to your collection, I've accomplished something.

through 2017

**starting in 1957*

ALBUMS
800-701

● ● ● ● ●

The 1960s, '70s, and '80s start earning their fair share, totaling 41 albums in this group. We meet a tortoise, some doves, a (snoop) dogg, and a deerhoof, along with albums called "The Lion and the Cobra", "Fishscale", and "The Hour of the Bewilderbeast".

800. "The Hour of Bewilderbeast", Badly Drawn Boy, 2000

799. "Faith", George Michael, 1987

798. "Slowhand", Eric Clapton, 1977

Plagued by inconsistency in nearly every iteration of his career, the guitar virtuoso penned and played his best solo songs, including "Wonderful Tonight" and "The Core", here. He shows up later in the countdown as part of Cream and Derek & the Dominos.

797. "Madman Across the Water", Elton John, 1971

796. "Fishscale", Ghostface Killah, 2006

795. "Process", Sampha, 2017

794. "Serena-Maneesh", Serena-Maneesh, 2005

793. "The Creek Drank the Cradle", Iron and Wine, 2002

792. "The Tyranny of Distance",
     Ted Leo & the Pharmacists, 2001

791. "Up to Anything", The Goon Sax, 2016

790. "London 0 Hull 4", The Housemartins, 1986

789. "The Raincoats", The Raincoats, 1979

788. "Red", King Crimson, 1974

> *"Red" joins "Starless and Bible Black" (see the next page) as one of two King Crimson albums released in 1974 on this list. After 1970, only Stevie Wonder (1972), Roxy Music (1973), and Belle and Sebastian (1996), in addition to King Crimson, accomplished this feat.*

787. "Check Your Head", Beastie Boys, 1992

786. "Raising Hell, Run-D.M.C., 1986

785. "Emperor Tomato Ketchup, Stereolab, 1996

784. "Quelqu'un M'a Dit", Carla Bruni, 2002

783. "Lateralus", Tool, 2001

782. "I Speak Because I Can", Laura Marling, 2010

781. "Wolfroy Goes to Town", Bonnie "Prince" Billy, 2011

780. "Damn the Torpedoes",
     Tom Petty & The Heartbreakers, 1979

779. "Friend Opportunity", Deerhoof, 2007

778. "Light Upon the Lake", Whitney, 2016

777. "The Boatman's Call",
Nick Cave & The Bad Seeds, 1997

776. "Bone Machine", Tom Waits, 1992

> Tom Waits scored top-1,000 points for albums released in the 1970s, '80s, and '90s. "Alice", from 2002, was a late cut. Only Bob Dylan contributes albums from four different decades to the list.

775. "Country Life", Roxy Music, 1974

774. "The Undertones", The Undertones, 1979

773. "A Night at the Opera", Queen, 1975

772. "Brilliant Corners", Thelonious Monk, 1957

771. "The Rhumb Line", Ra Ra Riot, 2008

770. "Starless and Bible Black", King Crimson, 1974

769. "A Swingin' Affair", Frank Sinatra, 1957

768. "Back in Black", AC/DC, 1980

767. "The Notorious Byrd Brothers", The Byrds, 1967

766. "Underwater Moonlight", The Soft Boys, 1980

765. "Burn Your Fire For No Witness", Angel Olsen, 2014

764. "Viva Last Blues", Palace Music, 1995

763. "Wincing the Night Away", The Shins, 2007

762. "Reachin' (A New Refutation of Time and Space)",
Digable Planets, 1993

761. "Tindersticks", Tindersticks, 1993

760. "The Psychedelic Furs", The Psychedelic Furs, 1980

759. "Room on Fire", The Strokes, 2003

758. "There Goes Rhymin' Simon", Paul Simon, 1973

757. "Kill 'em All", Metallica, 1983

756. "Goodbye and Hello", Tim Buckley, 1967

> *Jeff's dad was a tortured genius too, as evidenced by this psychedelic exploration of pleasure and pain. The title is a painful reminder of Buckley's death at 28, two years younger than the age at which his son would later perish.*

755. "TNT", Tortoise, 1998

754. "Ga Ga Ga Ga Ga", Spoon, 2007

753. "The Lion and the Cobra", Sinéad O'Connor, 1987

752. "Going to a Go-Go",
    Smokey Robinson and The Miracles, 1965

751. "Semper Femina", Laura Marling, 2017

750. "Spirit of Eden", Talk Talk, 1988

749. "Everybody Works", Jay Som, 2017

748. "Double Nickels on the Dime", Minutemen, 1984

747. "Visions", Grimes, 2012

746. "Appetite for Destruction", Guns N' Roses, 1987

745. "Go", Dexter Gordon, 1962

744. "Cypress Hill", Cypress Hill, 1991

743. "Down the River of Golden Dreams",
Okkervil River, 2003

742. "Strange Days", The Doors, 1967

741. "Deceit", This Heat, 1981

740. "Yuck", Yuck, 2011

739. "Let My Children Hear Music", Charles Mingus, 1972

> *Like all the jazz greats, Mingus peaked in the late '50s, but a decade and a half later, he was still blowing listeners' minds with work like "Let My Children Hear Music", the artist's personal favorite among his own output.*

738. "Eyelid Movies", Phantogram, 2009

737. "100 Days, 100 Nights",
Sharon Jones & The Dap-Kings, 2007

736. "untitled. unmastered.", Kendrick Lamar, 2016

735. "Future Days", Can, 1973

734. "Cape Dory", Tennis, 2011

733. "Before Today", Ariel Pink's Haunted Graffiti, 2010

732. "With a Little Help From My Friends",
Joe Cocker, 1969

731. "The Pleasure Principle", Gary Numan, 1979

730. "Sunbathing Animal", Parquet Courts, 2014

729. "Santana", Santana, 1969

728. "The Kick Inside", Kate Bush, 1978

727. "Old", Danny Brown, 2013

726. "Song Cycle", Van Dyke Parks, 1968

725. "Safe as Milk",
Captain Beefheart And His Magic Band, 1967

> *The often hilarious but impossibly dense "Trout Mask Replica" is often cited as Captain Beefheart's left-field masterpiece, but his debut is similarly quirky with a far richer sonic palette.*

724. "Far", Regina Spektor, 2009

723. "In Conflict", Owen Pallett, 2014

722. "Space is Only Noise", Nicolas Jaar, 2011

721. "Innerspeaker", Tame Impala, 2010

720. "A Moon Shaped Pool", Radiohead, 2016

719. "March of the Zapotec/Holland",
Beirut and Realpeople, 2009

718. "Green", R.E.M., 1988

717. "A Seat at the Table", Solange, 2016

716. "Doggystyle", Snoop Dogg, 1993

715. "The Incredible Jazz Guitar of Wes Montgomery", Wes Montgomery, 1960

714. "Black Messiah", D'Angelo and The Vanguard, 2014

713. "Smile", The Jayhawks, 2000

712. "Selling England by the Pound", Genesis, 1973

711. "Coin Coin Chapter One: Gens de Couleur Libres",
     Matana Roberts, 2011

710. "Blackstar", David Bowie, 2016

709. "Floating into the Night", Julee Cruise, 1989

708. "We Shall Overcome: The Seeger Sessions",
     Bruce Springsteen, 2006

707. "Bloom", Beach House, 2012

706. "Hallowed Ground", Violent Femmes, 1984

705. "The Slim Shady LP", Eminem, 1999

704. "Dookie", Green Day, 1994

703. "Lost Souls", Doves, 2000

702. "Beatles for Sale", The Beatles, 1964

701. "Green Onions", Booker T & the MGs, 1962

The house band for Stax Records scores an album of their own at #701. Stax labelmates Isaac Hayes, Big Star, and Otis Redding each recorded an album in the top 200.

WHAT MAKES PERFECT: PRACTICE OR PASSION?

● ● ● ● ●

A surgeon needs to study for a decade before cutting someone open. An athlete needs 15,000 reps to master her craft. Yet so many bands release their defining works in their early twenties, never to reach that pinnacle again.

Of the thousand albums on this list, 287 are debuts and 733 were released within five years of the artist's debut. Just 105 were released more than ten years into the artist's career.

While there are reasons to believe that a band's best chance to create a defining album is when it first signs with a label, a closer examination of those debut albums near the top of my list reveals that "debut" doesn't always mean "first attempt at songwriting". To wit:

Television's "Marquee Moon" came out in 1977, six years after Tom Verlaine founded The Neon Boys and four years after they added Richard Lloyd and became Television. Lloyd was still 25 when the album dropped, but Verlaine would turn 28 that year. Television suffered a typical sophomore slump with 1978's "Adventure" and then broke up, never having a chance to match their masterwork. Given the time the band spent playing together before "Marquee Moon" was released, it makes sense that they had more ideas and more time to hone them than they did in quickly turning around a follow-up album.

Arcade Fire's "Funeral" is the second debut on the list. Frontman Win Butler was just 24 when the album dropped. His wife and bandmate Régine Chassagne is three years older, but brother William is three years younger. Upon forming in 2003, Arcade Fire released a self-titled EP, but "Funeral" was written and recorded quickly and by a very young band. That said, Arcade Fire were no one-album wonder, as follow-up "Neon Bible" and Grammy Album of the Year "The Suburbs" nearly match the debut in intensity and artistry.

Next on the list of top debuts is "The Velvet Underground and Nico". Primary songwriters Lou Reed and John Cale each turned 25 the month the album was released. By the time they were 30, the band had broken up after releasing four wildly different yet consistently brilliant albums. Both went on to have long and successful music careers, but neither ever approached the genius of their VU days. Nico, meanwhile, was 28 and had already released singles on her own.

Rap supergroup Madvillain land the fourth debut on the list, "Madvillainy". "Debut" is perhaps the wrong word for this collaboration, as Daniel Dumile was 33 and had recorded as Zev Love X, MF Doom, Viktor Vaughn, and King Geedorah. Otis Jackson, Jr., was 30 and had recorded as Beat Konducta, Quasimoto, Malik Flavors, DJ Lord Such, the Loopdiggaz, and three solo albums as Madlib.

Similarly, Bonnie "Prince" Billy, whose debut under that moniker, "I See a Darkness", is next on the list, was no rookie. Will Oldham was 28 in 1999 and had recorded as Palace Music after a career as an actor. Still, he hasn't approached the perfection of "I See a Darkness" in a long and impressive solo career since its release.

Belle & Sebastian's "If You're Feeling Sinister" was released before, but recorded after "Tigermilk", a college project not initially intended for mass distribution. Whichever one considers the band's debut, it's clear that they did their best work in '96, when frontman Stuart Murdoch and Stevie Jackson were 27 and Isobel Campbell was just 20.

Led Zeppelin's self-titled debut ranks seventh among debuts, but just second among Led Zeppelin albums. The greats age well. Frontman Robert Plant was just 20 when the first album dropped and still just 32 when the band broke up late in 1980.

Derek & the Dominos are another super-group of well-established musicians, but King Crimson, Wu-Tang Clan, and Jeff Buckley all land legitimate debuts in the top 50 overall, with Fleet Foxes and The Cars (a shining example of peaking early) not far behind.

A counterexample of the early-peak phenomenon is Andrew Bird, who released his three best albums (at least in my estimation) in his thirties, having dabbled in every genre under the sun before locking down and mastering his sound. Miles Davis debuted in 1947, made the album widely regarded as the crown jewel of the genre in '59, and rewrote the language of jazz in the early '70s. Stevie Wonder recorded whatever Motown told him to as a teenager and kept the label alive throughout the '70s with classic after classic from his own mind.

Perhaps the year that did the most damage to the early-peak theory was 2016. First, 68-year-old David Bowie dropped "Blackstar", his best album in 40 years. Months later, and 48 years after his stunning debut, Leonard Cohen issued his best album since that one at 82 years old. Both died within weeks of the album release. Among the other artists who released top-1000 albums in 2016 were Nick Cave (59), Beyoncé (35), A Tribe Called Quest (26 years after forming), Radiohead (who formed in 1985, signed in '91, and debuted in '93), and a trio including 54-year-old k.d. Lang, 45-year-old Neko Case, and 42-year-old

Laura Veirs.

Are twenty-somethings better songwriters and musicians than thirty- and forty-somethings? Probably not. Scores of older artists are touring the world now, playing classics from their younger days with all the dexterity of their youth. The Grammys, for better or worse, keep giving Album of the Year awards to artists like Steely Dan and Beck, decades after critics and fans ate up their albums. The sophomore curse is likely a product of heightened expectations and less time to write and rehearse material once a band goes on tour to promote their debut.

Furthermore, listeners are always looking for something new, and critics love music that sounds fresh and breaks new ground. The canon of certified classics is loaded with albums like "Blue Lines" and "Endtroducing", which sounded like nothing before them, and albums like "The Cars" and "Is This It?" that fed nostalgia for a forgotten time.

Many artists run out of bold, groundbreaking material by thirty, but for every Jim Morrison or Ric Ocasek, there's a David Bowie or Leonard Cohen, rocking straight to the grave.

ALBUMS
700-601

● ● ● ● ●

This next group, while still dominated by 21st-century albums, includes 19 released in the 1970s. Heavy hitters Bob Dylan, Miles Davis, and R.E.M. all show up again, and we meet a Grizzly Bear, a Panda Bear, a Cat (Stevens), a Caribou, and a Cannibal Ox.

700. "Trailer Park", Beth Orton, 1996

699. "Brill Bruisers", The New Pornographers, 2014

698. "El Camino", The Black Keys, 2011

697. "Microcastle", Deerhunter, 2008

696. "I Am Not Afraid of You and I Will Beat Your Ass", Yo La Tengo, 2006

> *While my interest is limited to their livelier, more dynamic work like this one, others consider Yo La Tengo the American band with the greatest cumulative output, and I understand where they're coming from. "Pass the Hatchet, I Think I'm Goodkind" is 11 minutes of nirvana.*

695. "Rattus Norvegicus", The Stranglers, 1977

694. "Death Certificate", Ice Cube, 1991

693. "Yellow House", Grizzly Bear, 2006

692. "Two Suns", Bat for Lashes, 2009

691. "A Creature I Don't Know", Laura Marling, 2011

690. "With His Hot and Blue Guitar", Johnny Cash, 1957

689. "Rust Never Sleeps", Neil Young & Crazy Horse, 1979

Neil Young makes the list five times, twice crediting Crazy Horse as collaborators. While some of the material on "Rust Never Sleeps" was recorded live, it's all new material, so it's eligible for the list.

688. "Big Fish Theory", Vince Staples, 2017

687. "Love and Theft", Bob Dylan, 2001

686. "Learning to Crawl", Pretenders, 1984

685. "Modern Guilt", Beck, 2008

684. "Cosmo's Factory",
     Creedence Clearwater Revival, 1970

683. "The Meadowlands", The Wrens, 2003

682. "Solid Gold", Gang of Four, 1981

681. "Play", Moby, 1999

680. "The Smiths", The Smiths, 1984

679. "Too Rye Ay", Dexys Midnight Runners, 1982

678. "Scott 2", Scott Walker, 1968

677. "Station to Station", David Bowie, 1976

676. "All Eyez On Me", 2Pac, 1996

675. "Tupelo Honey", Van Morrison, 1971

674. "Steve McQueen", Prefab Sprout, 1985

673. "Little Earthquakes", Tori Amos, 1992

672. "Pink Moon", Nick Drake, 1972

671. "Person Pitch", Panda Bear, 2007

670. "Master of Reality", Black Sabbath, 1971

669. "Shadows on the Sun", Brother Ali, 2003

> *Certainly the only album on this list by an albino Muslim rapper from Minnesota, this one's worth the price of admission for "Forest Whitiker" alone, but it's consistently sharp and bold with a social conscience and skills to match.*

668. "Nilsson Schmilsson", Harry Nilsson, 1971

667. "Insignificance", Jim O'Rourke, 2001

666. "Suicide", Suicide, 1977

665. "Whatever and Ever Amen", Ben Folds Five, 1997

664. "Zombie", Fela Kuti & Africa 70, 1976

663. "Donuts", J. Dilla, 2006

662. "A Ghost is Born", Wilco, 2004

661. "Master of Puppets", Metallica, 1986

660. "Different Class", Pulp, 1995

659. "Supreme Clientele", Ghostface Killah, 2000

658. "This is Happening", LCD Soundsystem, 2010

657. "Midnite Vultures", Beck, 1999

656. "Arthur (or the Decline and Fall of the British Empire)", The Kinks, 1969

655. "Swim", Caribou, 2010

654. "Jolene", Dolly Parton, 1974

653. "True Love Cast Out All Evil", Roky Erickson & Okkervil River, 2010

> *Austin rockers Okkervil River contribute three other albums to this list, while Dallas-born Erickson shows up much later with his first band, The 13th Floor Elevators.*

652. "Trouble", Ray LaMontagne, 2004

651. "Black Sunday", Cypress Hill, 1993

650. "Vespertine", Björk, 2001

649. "The Payback", James Brown, 1973

648. "Ladies of the Canyon", Joni Mitchell, 1970

647. "Third", Portishead, 2008

646. "Raising Sand", Robert Plant & Alison Krauss, 2007

645. "Teaser and the Firecat", Cat Stevens, 1971

644. "Miles Smiles", Miles Davis, 1967

643. "Helplessness Blues", Fleet Foxes, 2011

642. "Baduizm", Erykah Badu, 1997

641. "Rated R", Queens of the Stone Age, 2000

640. "Traffic", Traffic, 1968

639. "The Stone Roses", The Stone Roses, 1989

638. "Halo", Juana Molina, 2017

> *Argentinian singer/songwriter Juana Molina recorded her richest and most sonically diverse album 26 years into her career. 2008's "Un Día" is nearly its equal.*

637. "A Church That Fits Our Needs",
Lost in the Trees, 2012

636. "Can't Buy a Thrill", Steely Dan, 1972

635. "The Stooges", The Stooges, 1969

634. "case/lang/viers", Case/Lang/Viers, 2016

633. "Gorillaz", Gorillaz, 2001

632. "American Idiot", Green Day, 2004

631. "American Dream", LCD Soundsystem, 2017

630. "Melody of Certain Damaged Lemons",
Blonde Redhead, 2000

629. "Gish", The Smashing Pumpkins, 1991

628. "Entertainment!", Gang of Four, 1979

627. "Meat is Murder", The Smiths, 1985

626. "Painted Shut", Hop Along, 2015

625. "Getz/Gilberto", Stan Getz & João Gilberto, 1963

> *Stan Getz lands two collaborations in the top 1,000, with a solo album on the honorable mention list. You know "Girl From Ipanema", but the rest of this collaboration, the high point of Getz's samba phase, is similarly strong.*

624. "Pieces of the Sky", Emmylou Harris, 1975

623. "Repeater", Fugazi, 1990

622. "Think of One", Wynton Marsalis, 1983

621. "Psychocandy", The Jesus and Mary Chain, 1985

620. "Yellow Moon", The Neville Brothers, 1989

619. "The Cold Vein", Cannibal Ox, 2001

618. "Apologies to the Queen Mary", Wolf Parade, 2005

617. "My Generation", The Who, 1965

616. "Heaven or Las Vegas", Cocteau Twins, 1990

615. "On Avery Island", Neutral Milk Hotel, 1996

614. "You're Dead!", Flying Lotus, 2014

613. "The Wall", Pink Floyd, 1979

612. "Dear Catastrophe Waitress", Belle & Sebastian, 2003

611. "Shields", Grizzly Bear, 2012

610. "Oar", Alexander "Skip" Spence, 1969

609. "Fulfillingness' First Finale", Stevie Wonder, 1974

608. "Chet!", Chet Baker, 1959

607. "Come Away With Me", Norah Jones, 2002

606. "Fleetwood Mac", Fleetwood Mac, 1975

605. "Let Them Eat Chaos", Kate Tempest, 2016

604. "Daybreaker", Beth Orton, 2002

603. "An Awesome Wave", Alt-J, 2012

602. "Son con Guaguancó", Celia Cruz, 1966

> *"Son Con Guaguancó", the best album by Ursula Hilaria Celia de la Caridad Cruz Alfonso de la Santisima Trinidad, is probably the only album on this list one would file under "salsa".*

601. "Mother Juno", The Gun Club, 1987

VICTIMS OF THE RULES

● ● ● ● ●

The last 100 albums featured lone contributions from Johnny Cash and Chet Baker, two artists who deserved better. Cash was limited by my prohibition of live albums, while Baker suffered from my 1957 cutoff. Following are some albums that would certainly have made my list (with approximate position in parenthesis) if not for various rules. This is not necessarily an exhaustive list, as a focus on older albums, live albums, or EPs would have extended the scope of this project beyond what I could possibly have absorbed. That said, each of these albums held a spot on this list at some point before the final lines were drawn:

Pre-1957:

"In the Wee Small Hours", Frank Sinatra, 1955 (75)

"Chet Baker Sings", Chet Baker, 1954 (100)

"Elvis Presley", Elvis Presley, 1956 (300)

"Songs for Swinging Lovers", Frank Sinatra, 1955 (320)

"Saxophone Colossus", Sonny Rollins, 1956 (770)

"Sarah Vaughan", Sarah Vaughan, 1954 (995)

Live Albums:

"At Folsom Prison", Johnny Cash, 1968 (45)

"Live at the Apollo", James Brown, 1963 (95)

"MTV Unplugged in New York", Nirvana, 1994 (225)

"Sunday at the Village Vanguard", Bill Evans Trio, 1961 (900)

EPs (non-full-length):

"Lesson No. 1", Glenn Branca, 1980 (210)

"Kindred", Burial, 2012 (460)

"Harmony of Difference", Kamasi Washington, 2017 (510)

ALBUMS
600-501

● ● ● ● ●

The just-missed-the-top-500 group is dominated by weirdness, with Nico, Laurie Anderson, Kraftwerk, and Deafheaven pushing the limits of what one might call music. Michael Jackson and Madonna are here to inject some accessibility, and Spoon and The Knife may help you get it all down.

600. "Spiderland", Slint, 1991

599. "Ege Bamyasi", Can, 1972

> *Can's fourth album eschewed 20-minute freakouts in favor of more accessible songs, peaking with "Vitamin C", the best song the German group ever recorded.*

598. "The Carnival", Wyclef Jean, 1997

597. "Pata Pata", Miriam Makeba, 1967

596. "Another Side of Bob Dylan", Bob Dylan, 1964

595. "Sleeping Through the War", All Them Witches, 2017

594. "Only Built for Cuban Linx", Raekwon, 1995

593. "To Bring You My Love", PJ Harvey, 1995

592. "Paul Simon", Paul Simon, 1972

591. "Fuzzy Logic", Super Furry Animals, 1996

590. "All Hour Cymbals", Yeasayer, 2007

589. "You & Me", The Walkmen, 2008

588. "Modern Sounds in Country & Western Music", Ray Charles, 1962

587. "Juju", Siouxsie and the Banshees, 1981

586. "A Tribute to Jack Johnson", Miles Davis, 1971

585. "The Underside of Power", Algiers, 2017

584. "Puberty 2", Mitski, 2016

> *Mitski is one of a handful of artists on this list who would almost certainly add another album ("Be the Cowboy") if I included those released in 2018. Others would probably include Janelle Monae, Deafheaven, and Kamasi Washington.*

583. "3 Years, 5 Months and 2 Days in the Life of...", Arrested Development, 1992

582. "Extraordinary Machine", Fiona Apple, 2005

581. "Visions of a Life", Wolf Alice, 2017

580. "Something More than Free", Jason Isbell, 2015

579. "Document", R.E.M., 1987

578. "Black Sabbath", Black Sabbath, 1970

577. "It Was Hot, We Stayed in the Water",
     The Microphones, 2000

576. "Keep it Like a Secret", Built to Spill, 1999

575. "Foxbase Alpha", Saint Etienne, 1991

574. "Fresh Cream", Cream, 1966

573. "His Band and the Street Choir", Van Morrison, 1970

572. "Lanquidity", Sun Ra & His Arkestra, 1978

571. "True Blue", Madonna, 1986

Critical appeal was more in vogue with later Madonna albums, but the first album on which she at least shares a writing credit on every song is her masterpiece, loaded with timeless pop songs with heart and, in several cases, depth.

570. "Green River", Creedence Clearwater Revival, 1969

569. "Lust for Life", Iggy Pop, 1977

568. "Off the Wall", Michael Jackson, 1979

567. "Zenyatta Mondatta", The Police, 1980

566. "Kill the Moonlight", Spoon, 2002

565. "Surf", Donnie Trumpet &
     The Social Experiment, 2015

564. "Guero", Beck, 2005

563. "w h o k i l l" tUnE-yArDs, 2011

562. "Tijuana Moods", Charles Mingus, 1962

561. "Aladdin Sane", David Bowie, 1973

560. "Outlandos d'Amour", The Police, 1978

559. "Malibu", Anderson .Paak, 2016

558. "The Earth is Not a Cold Dead Place",
Explosions in the Sky, 2003

557. "Clap Your Hands Say Yeah",
Clap Your Hands Say Yeah, 2005

556. "The Sensual World", Kate Bush, 1989

555. "Cold Fact", Rodriguez, 1970

554. "Guppy", Charly Bliss, 2017

553. "Primrose Green", Ryley Walker, 2015

552. "Blur", Blur, 1997

> *"Blur" is one of 58 self-titled albums on this list. Not surprisingly, 44 of those represent the artist's debut. Blur released a list-high four albums before self-titling one. Fleetwood Mac and The Beatles each released ten studio albums before the one on this list, but they'd both dabbled in self-titling earlier in their careers.*

551. "Chicago" (II), Chicago, 1970

550. "Dry", PJ Harvey, 1992

549. "Sail Away", Randy Newman, 1972

548. "Perfect From Now On", Built to Spill, 1997

547. "New Bermuda", Deafheaven, 2015

546. "Os Mutantes", Os Mutantes, 1968

545. "Ladies and Gentlemen We Are Floating in Space",
Spiritualized, 1997

544. "Silent Shout", The Knife, 2006

543. "Real Life", Magazine, 1978

542. "Architect", C Duncan, 2015

541. "Carnavas", Silversun Pickups, 2006

540. "The Piper at the Gates of Dawn", Pink Floyd, 1967

539. "Another Green World", Brian Eno, 1975

538. "Close to the Edge", Yes, 1972

537. "A Northern Soul", The Verve, 1995

536. "Heart Like a Wheel", Linda Ronstadt, 1974

535. "With Light and Love", Woods, 2014

534. "Achtung Baby", U2, 1991

533. "Tanglewood Numbers", Silver Jews, 2005

> *I may be on an island completely to myself in liking "late" Silver Jews, as all of David Berman's recordings between 1998 and 2005, but no earlier albums, land on the list. "Punks in the Beerlight" is sublime.*

532. "Bizarre Ride II the Pharcyde", The Pharcyde, 1992

531. "Los Angeles", X, 1980

530. "Today", Galaxie 500, 1988

529. "Transgender Dysphoria Blues", Against Me!, 2014

528. "Scott 4," Scott Walker, 1969

527. "Infinite Worlds", Vagabon, 2017

526. "The Great Escape", Blur, 1995

525. "Nothing's Shocking", Jane's Addiction, 1988

524. "XTRMNTR", Primal Scream, 2000

523. "More Than Any Other Day", Ought, 2014

522. "Axis: Bold as Love",
    The Jimi Hendrix Experience, 1967

521. "Screamadelica", Primal Scream, 1991

520. "Sound Affects, The Jam 1980

519. "Circulatory System", Circulatory System, 2001

518. "The Trials of Van Occupanther", Midlake, 2006

517. "Idlewild South", The Allman Brothers Band, 1970

516. "Head Over Heels", Cocteau Twins, 1983

> *Cocteau Twins rank ninth in Rank Points in the 1980s, but if we redefine the decade as 1981-1990, they move up to sixth, behind only R.E.M., Sonic Youth, The Smiths, Pixies, and The Replacements.*

515. "Liege and Lief", Fairpoint Convention, 1969

514. "I Am the Fun Blame Monster", Menomena, 2003

513. "Foil Deer", Speedy Ortiz, 2015

512. "The Mysterious Production of Eggs",
    Andrew Bird, 2005

511. "We Are the 21st Century Ambassadors of Peace
    and Magic", Foxygen, 2013

510. "Days of Future Passed", The Moody Blues, 1967

509. "Blood, Sweat, & Tears", Blood, Sweat, & Tears, 1969

508. "Two Steps from the Blues", Bobby "Blue" Bland, 1961

507. "Psyence Fiction", UNKLE, 1998

506. "Stay Positive", The Hold Steady, 2008

505. "Trans Europa Express", Kraftwerk, 1977

504. "Big Science, Laurie Anderson, 1982

503. "Unknown Pleasures, Joy Division, 1979

502. "Boy in Da Corner, Dizzee Rascal, 2003

> *There's a lot of hip-hop on this list and almost all of it is American. This witty, skillful Mercury Prize winner is the countdown's highest-ranking British rap album.*

501. "Desertshore", Nico, 1970

MY FAVORITE ALBUM FROM EVERY YEAR
PART I

* * * * *

Here's my favorite album released in each year between 1957 and 1987.

1957-1964:
Rock 'n' roll is born, but jazz still reigns.

1957: "Blue Train", John Coltrane
Despite breakouts from Little Richard and Buddy Holly, jazz still ruled the day in '57.

1958: "Somethin' Else", Cannonball Adderley
While Miles and Coltrane innovated, Cannonball made impeccable pop jazz. No non-jazz album from '58 cracked the list.

1959: "Kind of Blue", Miles Davis
In perhaps the art form's best year, Miles easily tops the five '59 jazz albums on the list.

1960: "At Last!", Etta James
A thrilling album in a dud of a year (just four albums make the list), rhythm and blues finally wins one

1961: "Workout", Hank Mobley
This high-energy jazz romp is a worthy champ in one of the weakest years of the study.

1962: "Tijuana Moods", Charles Mingus
At #531, the lowest-ranked album-of-the-year on the list, but it beats out some early rock classics. Ray Charles and Oscar Peterson highlight a great year for the piano.

1963: "The Black Saint and the Sinner Lady", Charles Mingus
The Beatles debut and Dylan breaks through, but Mingus hits us with his masterpiece.

1964: "The Sidewinder", Lee Morgan
A British invasion rocks the USA, but an irresistible jazz album takes the prize.

1965-1973:
Dylan plugs in, the British invade, and rock takes the throne.

1965: "Highway 61 Revisited", Bob Dylan
Folk goes electric and the rules are changed forever; this is the first year with more than ten albums in my top 1,000.

1966: "Pet Sounds", The Beach Boys
Thirteen albums make the list and the Beach Boys' nostalgia-tinged pop with harmonies from heaven edges out masterworks by Dylan and The Beatles.

1967: "The Velvet Underground and Nico", The Velvet Underground
Sgt. Pepper, Aretha, Love, and Jimi make strong bids, but this strangely beautiful flirtation with everything lurking down that dark alley carries a great year.

1968: "Electric Ladyland", The Jimi Hendrix Experience
With apologies to the Beatles, Stones, and everyone else, Hendrix owned the summer of love.

1969: "Abbey Road", The Beatles
In the most represented year in the study, this narrowly defeats the Stones' best and stunning debuts from Led Zeppelin and King Crimson.

1970: "After the Gold Rush", Neil Young
A fitting winner in the year of the singer/songwriter, Neil tops Nick Drake, Elton John, and Cat Stevens.

1971: "Blue", Joni Mitchell
Joni beats Janis and all the guys in another strong year.

1972: "Exile on Main Street", The Rolling Stones
The competition starts to dwindle, but the Stones will not fade away.

1973: "Innervisions", Stevie Wonder
As rock enters hibernation, Stevie gives us maybe the best R&B album ever. Early works by Roxy Music, Springsteen, and Tom Waits herald a new guard.

1974-1981:
Rock gets bloated, punk fills the void.

1974: "Pretzel Logic", Steely Dan
The only year between '69 and '80 not to feature a top-200 album, this jazz-flavored pop record leads a field of strange gems.

1975: "Physical Graffiti", Led Zeppelin
After four top-eight finishes, Zeppelin finally claims the

top spot over a young Patti Smith and a less-young Bob Dylan.

1976: "The Ramones", The Ramones
A year ahead of punk's heyday, The Ramones arrive. Nobody else did much of anything.

1977: "Marquee Moon", Television
...and Television quickly turns punk inside-out with guitar heroics, beating out Fleetwood Mac's drama and Wire's paranoia.

1978: "The Cars", The Cars
Homage to fifties pop was de rigueur in '78 and The Cars did it better than Elvis Costello or Blondie.

1979: "London Calling", The Clash
Right before punk jumps the shark, The Clash throw it in a blender with every other genre, beating out Talking Heads and two albums about walls.

1980: "Pretenders", Pretenders
My birth year was a slow one for music, but Pretenders' debut would be a contender in most any year.

1981: "Fire of Love", The Gun Club
Brian Eno and David Byrne conspire to take the throne, but the Gun Club's debut wins the duel.

1982-1987:
Pop reigns the airwaves while the underground rebels.

1982: "Thriller", Michael Jackson
Disco is dead, punk is hiding underground, and traditional rock is limited to Springsteen and his ilk. If not for the King of Pop, this year would be a total washout.

1983: "Synchronicity", The Police
In a bit of a rebound year, The Police narrowly edge R.E.M. and the Violent Femmes.

1984: "Let it Be", The Replacements
The mid-'80s belonged to The Replacements, who'll finish in the top 20 two more times, and R.E.M., who finish a close second for the second straight year.

1985: "Rain Dogs", Tom Waits
In a sea of straightforward pop, the weird stand out. The 35-year-old Waits, the oldest solo winner of this award except Mingus, tops Kate Bush and Hüsker Dü.

1986: "The Queen is Dead", The Smiths
Pop reclaims the throne, with The Smiths topping Paul Simon, Peter Gabriel, and Madonna. It's the third of four straight years The Smiths finish in the top ten.

1987: "The Joshua Tree", U2
Perhaps my least-favorite acclaimed band delivers their best album in a lackluster year.

ALBUMS
500-401

● ● ● ● ●

This is the first group of 100 to include three albums from the eligible portion of the 1950s, courtesy of Buddy Holly, Ornette Coleman, and Miles Davis. One of those three artists is far from done. Bruce Springsteen and Nick Cave match that decade's output here.

500. "Led Zeppelin III", Led Zeppelin, 1970

499. "Mosaic", Art Blakey & the Jazz Messengers, 1961

498. "Radio City", Big Star, 1974

497. "Out of Time", R.E.M., 1991

This is where my R.E.M. fixation rings like the guitars on "Murmur". The four R.E.M. albums ahead of this one on the list are all, to various degrees, well-regarded critically. This one gets dragged for overambition and overproduction, but "Country Feedback" and "Low" are perfect and every song on the album stays in your head for days.

496. "I Should Coco", Supergrass, 1995

495. "Ta Det Lungt", Dungen, 2004

494. "100 Miles and Running", Wale, 2007

493. "Illuminations", Buffy Sainte-Marie, 1969

492. "Lousy With Sylvianbriar", Of Montreal, 2013

491. "Desire", Bob Dylan, 1976

490. "Desire", Pharoahe Monch, 2007

489. "On Fire", Galaxie 500, 1989

488. "EVOL", Sonic Youth, 1986

487. "Bon Iver, Bon Iver", Bon Iver, 2011

486. "Blue Cathedral", Comets on Fire, 2004

> *These two "Desires" don't have much in common aside from their titles. Dylan was a decade in, having mastered folk and rock and started to explore county by '76. Monch was almost two decades into a rap career and hadn't released a solo album in 8 years in '07.*

485. "Kala", M.I.A., 2007

484. "Giant Steps", The Boo Radleys, 1993

483. "Art Angels", Grimes, 2015

482. "People's Instinctive Travels and the Paths of Rhythm", A Tribe Called Quest, 1990

481. "Smile", Brian Wilson, 2004

480. "Bookends", Simon & Garfunkel, 1968

479. "Shoot Out the Lights", Richard & Linda Thompson, 1982

478. "Elliott Smith", Elliott Smith, 1995

477. "Let Love In", Nick Cave & The Bad Seeds, 1994

> *Nick and the Seeds, who debuted in 1984, land albums in the top 1,000 recorded in the '90s, '00s, and '10s, but none from the '80s (though "Tender Prey" gets an honorable mention), a rarity in an industry where youth is such an asset.*

476. "Fox Confessor Brings the Flood", Neko Case, 2006

475. "Born to Run", Bruce Springsteen, 1975

474. "The Times They Are A-Changin'", Bob Dylan, 1964

473. "You're Living All Over Me", Dinosaur, Jr., 1987

472. "Untrue", Burial, 2007

471. "Call the Doctor", Sleater-Kinney, 1996

470. "Nebraska", Bruce Springsteen, 1982

469. "Wish You Were Here", Pink Floyd, 1975

468. "Post", Björk, 1995

467. "Begin to Hope", Regina Spektor, 2006

466. "Fresh Fruit for Rotting Vegetables", Dead Kennedys, 1980

465. "Honky Tonk Heroes", Waylon Jennings, 1973

464. "Twelve Dreams of Dr. Sardonicus", Spirit, 1970

463. "Modern Vampires of the City", Vampire Weekend, 2013

462. "Transformer", Lou Reed, 1972

461. "Honky Chateau", Elton John, 1972

460. "Round About Midnight", Miles Davis, 1957

459. "We Got It From Here... Thank You 4 Your Service",
A Tribe Called Quest, 2016

> *A Tribe Called Quest lands two albums released 26 years apart within 25 spots of each other. The only other artists with two albums covering such a time span anywhere on the list are Bob Dylan, Bruce Springsteen, David Bowie, and Leonard Cohen.*

458. "Turn on the Bright Lights", Interpol, 2002

457. "A Love Supreme", John Coltrane, 1965

456. "You Want it Darker", Leonard Cohen, 2016

455. "Metal Box", Public Image Ltd., 1979

454. "Sketches of Spain", Miles Davis, 1960

453. "Plans", Death Cab for Cutie, 2005

452. "Debut", Björk, 1993

451. "HEAL", Strand of Oaks, 2014

450. "Willy and the Poor Boys",
Creedence Clearwater Revival, 1969

449. "Cheap Thrills",
Big Brother & The Holding Company, 1968

448. "Pronounced Leh-Nerd Skin-Nerd",
Lynyrd Skynyrd, 1973

447. "Meat Puppets II", Meat Puppets, 1984

446. "Damn", Kendrick Lamar, 2017

445. "3 Feet High and Rising", De La Soul, 1989

444. "The Shepherd's Dog", Iron and Wine, 2007

443. "The Shape of Jazz to Come", Ornette Coleman, 1959

442. "Takk..", Sigur Rós, 2005

The consummate critic's darling, Sigur Rós first courted popular appeal on their fifth full-length with relative pop fare like "Glósóli" and "Hoppipolla", sacrificing none of the angelic sound that landed them in the final pages of this book.

441. "Speakerboxxx/The Love Below", OutKast, 2003

440. "Album", Girls, 2009

439. "The Kinks are the Village Green Preservation Society", The Kinks, 1968

438. "Lift Your Skinny Fists Like Antennas to Heaven", Godspeed You! Black Emperor, 2000

437. "The Lamb Lies Down on Broadway", Genesis, 1974

436. "A Rush of Blood to the Head", Coldplay, 2002

435. "Skeleton Tree", Nick Cave & The Bad Seeds, 2016

434. "Disintegration", The Cure, 1989

433. "The Stranger", Billy Joel, 1977

432. "Mr. Tambourine Man", The Byrds, 1965

431. "Mercy, Mercy, Mercy!", Cannonball Adderley, 1966

430. "Tronic", Black Milk, 2008

429. "Electro-Shock Blues", Eels, 1998

428. "Quality", Talib Kweli, 2002

427. "The 'Chirping' Crickets",
Buddy Holly & His Crickets, 1957

426. "Fifth Dimension", The Byrds, 1966

> *"Fifth Dimension" edges out Byrds debut "Mr. Tambourine Man" not because it sounds better, but because the band started trusting their own instincts with original songs like "Eight Miles High" and "Mr. Spaceman", rather than letting Bob Dylan do half of their songwriting.*

425. "The Holy Bible", Manic Street Preachers, 1994

424. "Sun Structures", Temples, 2014

423. "Maxinquaye", Tricky, 1995

422. "Oh, Inverted World!", The Shins, 2001

421. "Court and Spark", Joni Mitchell, 1974

420. "Dirty", Sonic Youth, 1992

419. "Lemonade", Beyoncé, 2016

418. "Ride the Lightning", Metallica, 1984

417. "Thunder, Lightning, Strike", The Go! Team, 2004

416. "Black on Both Sides", Mos Def, 1999

415. "Wolfgang Amadeus Phoenix", Phoenix, 2009

414. "Time (The Revelator)", Gillian Welch, 2001

413. "American Water", Silver Jews, 1998

412. "Paid in Full", Eric B. & Rakim, 1987

411. "Discipline", King Crimson, 1981

410. "Sunbather", Deafheaven, 2013

> *While other bands with albums on this list like My Bloody Valentine, Ride, The Verve, and Slowdive may also operate within the shoegaze genre, only the two Deafheaven albums (and maybe the one below) might also be found in the black metal section of your local record store.*

409. "Ecailles de Lune", Alcest, 2010

408. "New View", Eleanor Friedberger, 2016

407. "The Order of Time", Valerie June, 2017

406. "Mothership Connection", Parliament, 1975

405. "Dig!!! Lazarus Dig!!!",
Nick Cave & The Bad Seeds, 2008

404. "The Trinity Session", Cowboy Junkies, 1988

403. "Bakesale", Sebadoh, 1994

402. "Born in the U.S.A.", Bruce Springsteen, 1984

401. "Rufus Wainwright", Rufus Wainwright, 1998

MY FAVORITE ALBUM FROM EVERY YEAR
PART II

* * * * *

Here's my favorite album released in each year between 1988 and 2017.

1988-1996:
Rock goes alternative and hip-hop takes off.

1988: "Daydream Nation", Sonic Youth
Peers Pixies and Dinosaur, Jr. put up a good fight, as do hip-hop acts like Public Enemy, EMPD, and N.W.A., but this is Sonic Youth's only win.

1989: "Doolittle", Pixies
Pixies win by a solid margin over the second-place Beastie Boys, as the rest of the rap game takes a year off to dig for samples.

1990: "Ritual de lo Habitual", Jane's Addiction
A bilingual joyride from a band that might have ruled the world if they'd lasted a little longer, this tops innovations in jazz-based hip-hop, shoegaze, and post-hardcore.

1991: "Loveless", My Bloody Valentine
Grunge took over with Nirvana's and Pearl Jam's ascension, but MBV made the biggest statement.

1992: "Automatic for the People", R.E.M.
The best band of the '80s finally gets its title a decade after landing a top-15 album seven years in a row.

1993: "Enter the Wu-Tang (36 Chambers)", Wu-Tang Clan
Hip-hop finally gets its due, topping Liz Phair's masterpiece, in a year when Britpop and grunge were duking it out across the Atlantic.

1994: "Crooked Rain, Crooked Rain", Pavement
In maybe the best year ever for debut albums, Pavement's second beats out firsts by Jeff Buckley, Nas, Portishead, Weezer, and The Notorious B.I.G.

1995: "The Bends", Radiohead
Radiohead's second album was just a hint of what was to come, but it's enough to beat out another Pavement classic and the best work by Oasis and Elastica.

1996: "If You're Feeling Sinister", Belle & Sebastian
Belle & Sebastian become the only artist to hold the top two spots in any year, beating out Beck, R.E.M., and Jay-Z.

1997-2005:
Technology emboldens the rock formula and the language is expanded.

1997: "OK Computer", Radiohead
Some would argue Radiohead were still warming up, but this is their last album-of-the-year. Runner-up Björk's "Homogenic" holds a similar place in the art-rock canon.

1998: "In the Aeroplane Over the Sea", Neutral Milk Hotel
In a fantastic year for experimental music that featured OutKast, Mercury Rev, and Amon Tobin, the kings of weird take the prize.

1999: "I See a Darkness", Bonnie "Prince" Billy
If this book leads you to buy one album, this should probably be it, though Sigur Rós, Fiona Apple, and The Flaming Lips put out all-timers in '99 too.

2000: "Stankonia", OutKast
It takes maybe the best hip-hop album ever to knock Radiohead to number two in a strong year.

2001: "Is This It?" The Strokes
The second (or is it first?) year of the new millennium drops off significantly from the prior year, but The Strokes and Stripes both deliver.

2002: "Yankee Hotel Foxtrot", Wilco
It takes a left-field classic to top timeless albums by Beck and The Flaming Lips.

2003: "Elephant", The White Stripes
This is vindication for the Stripes after a second-place finish in '01, edging out The Shins, Caribou, and The Yeah Yeah Yeahs.

2004: "Funeral", Arcade Fire
"Funeral" wins, but only The Stones' "Let it Bleed" ranks higher on the overall list than Madvillain's "Madvillainy" without winning its year.

2005: "Illinoise", Sufjan Stevens
In a deep and top-heavy year, Sufjan's second entry in his soon-after-aborted fifty states project beats Kanye,

Okkervil, and Antony.

2006-2017:
The album fades as an art form,
but brilliant music still abounds

2006: "Back to Black", Amy Winehouse
The Decemberists land one of their three top-five
albums in '06, but they can't top Amy.

2007: "Armchair Apocrypha", Andrew Bird
An underappreciated album by an underappreciated
artists tops an underappreciated year in which Of
Montreal, LCD Soundsystem, Bon Iver, and Jens
Lekman all deliver their best work.

2008: "Fleet Foxes", Fleet Foxes
This is the easiest call of the decade, both because this
Americana landmark is so good and because '08 takes
a nose dive after a bunch of great years.

2009: "Veckatimest", Grizzly Bear
In the year I started making year-end lists, Dirty
Projectors won my praise, but I've since warmed further
to Grizzly Bear and the debut by The XX.

2010: "My Beautiful Dark Twisted Fantasy", Kanye West
He's off his rocker, but this album is proof that there
was once a Stevie Wonder-level genius in that head.
Deerhunter, Arcade Fire, The Black Keys, and The
National were great in '10 too.

2011: "Civilian", Wye Oak
This is the weakest year of the decade so far, but Wye
Oak delivered a strong contender for album of the
decade and The Decemberists weren't far behind.

2012: "Good Kid, M.A.A.D. City", Kendrick Lamar
Despite competition from Frank Ocean, Tame Impala, and the ageless Andrew Bird, a new king ascends to his throne.

2013: "Muchacho", Phosphorescent
There's not much competition in '13, but aside from the record above, this is the album of the decade so far.

2014: "Are We There", Sharon Van Etten
With three wildly different albums, this is the only year in the study in which women hold the top three spots (St. Vincent and Wye Oak are the others).

2015: "To Pimp a Butterfly", Kendrick Lamar
Only Mingus, Radiohead, and Kendrick win two years, though Sufjan Stevens just missed here.

2016: "Teens of Denial", Car Seat Headrest
A 23-year-old singing about high school rules the year of the elder (see "Practice or Passion").

2017: "The Navigator", Hurray for the Riff Raff
Alynda Segarra's odes to her New York City life and Puerto Rican roots claim the last year of the study.

ALBUMS
400-301

● ● ● ● ●

The 1970s make a strong effort here, landing 28 of these 100 albums, as do the 2000s, with 21. This is also the only group of 100 to feature three country albums, thanks to Willie Nelson, Lucinda Williams, and Kacey Musgraves.

400. "Wish Someone Would Care," Irma Thomas, 1964

399. "On the Corner", Miles Davis, 1972

398. "The Lonesome Crowded West", Modest Mouse, 1997

397. "Shriek", Wye Oak, 2014

396. "Chairs Missing", Wire, 1978

> *Wire's second (and second-best) album picked up right where their stunning debut left off, though they added some extended workouts to the sub-two-minute punk nuggets like "Outdoor Miner" they perfected the first time around.*

395. "déjà vu", Crosby, Stills, Nash & Young, 1970

394. "Seven Swans", Sufjan Stevens, 2004

393. "Rocket to Russia", Ramones, 1977

392. "Vaudeville Villain", Viktor Vaughn, 2003

391. "Dig Your Own Hole", The Chemical Brothers, 1997

390. "Same Trailer, Different Park",
     Kacey Musgraves, 2013

389. "My Aim is True", Elvis Costello, 1977

388. "The Band", The Band, 1968

387. "Love and Hate", Michael Kiwanuka, 2016

386. "Time Out of Mind", Bob Dylan, 1997

> *Bob Dylan released albums that appear in the top 700 of this list in the 1960s, '70s, '90s, and 2000s. This is the only won that won the Album of the Year Grammy.*

385. "Giant Steps", John Coltrane, 1960

384. "I'm Still in Love With You", Al Green, 1972

383. "Curtis", Curtis Mayfield, 1970

382. "The Colour of Spring", Talk Talk, 1986

381. "Random Access Memories", Daft Punk, 2013

380. "Rook", Shearwater, 2008

379. "Carwheels on a Gravel Road",
     Lucinda Williams, 1998

378. "Fear of Music", Talking Heads, 1979

377. "Small Change", Tom Waits, 1976

376. "Endtroducing", DJ Shadow, 1996

375. "Oracular Spectacular", MGMT, 2007

374. "Tago Mago", Can, 1971

373. "Abraxas", Santana, 1970

372. "The Eminem Show", Eminem, 2002

371. "Silence Yourself", Savages, 2013

370. "Maggot Brain", Funkadelic, 1971

369. "Red Headed Stranger", Willie Nelson, 1975

> *No other artist tried harder to make this list, basically releasing an album a year throughout the eligible time period. At the peak of his powers in the mid-'70s, Willie struck gold twice, peaking with this big-hearted take on outlaw country.*

368. "Vampire Weekend", Vampire Weekend, 2008

367. "Poses", Rufus Wainwright, 2001

366. "Superfly", Curtis Mayfield, 1972

365. "Girls Can Tell", Spoon, 2001

364. "Demon Days", Gorillaz, 2005

363. "Time Out", Dave Brubeck Quartet, 1959

362. "Strangeways, Here We Come", The Smiths, 1987

361. "Beauty and the Beat", Edan, 2005

> *88 of 92 hip-hop albums on the list come from American artists. New York, Los Angeles, Chicago, Philadelphia, Detroit, and Atlanta are well represented. Only Edan, who was born in Maryland, made his name rapping in Boston.*

360. "Saturdays=Youth", M83, 2008

359. "There's a Riot Goin' On", Sly & The Family Stone, 1971

358. "The Epic", Kamasi Washington, 2015

357. "Workout", Hank Mobley, 1961

356. "XO", Elliott Smith, 1998

355. "No Other", Gene Clark, 1974

354. "St. Vincent", St. Vincent, 2014

353. "Good News for People Who Love Bad News", Modest Mouse, 2004

352. "Eat a Peach", The Allman Brothers Band, 1972

351. "Songs in the Key of Life", Stevie Wonder, 1976

350. "Mass Romantic", The New Pornographers, 2000

349. "Bug", Dinosaur, Jr., 1988

348. "Harvest", Neil Young, 1972

347. "A Hard Day's Night", The Beatles, 1964

346. "Magical Mystery Tour", The Beatles, 1967

345. "Third/Sister Lovers", Big Star, 1978

344. "Food and Liquor", Lupe Fiasco, 2006

343. "Straight Outta Compton", N.W.A., 1988

342. "So", Peter Gabriel, 1986

341. "Stand Up", Jethro Tull, 1969

When flute rock failed to take off and Grammy voters mistook their later music for heavy metal, Jethro Tull became something of a punchline. Anyone willing to scour their back catalog from the years before they started writing album-length songs will be rewarded with this bit of classic rock perfection.

340. "13", Blur, 1999

339. "My Life in the Bush of Ghosts",
     Brian Eno & David Byrne, 1981

338. "69 Love Songs", The Magnetic Fields, 1999

337. "Have One on Me", Joanna Newsom, 2010

336. "Attack on Memory", Cloud Nothings, 2012

335. "Closing Time", Tom Waits, 1973

334. "Destroyer's Rubies", Destroyer, 2006

333. "Crazy Rhythms", Feelies, 1980

332. "Visiter", The Dodos, 2008

331. "What Color is Love?", Terry Callier, 1972

330. "Talking Book", Stevie Wonder, 1972

329. "Midnight Marauders", A Tribe Called Quest, 1993

328. "Surrealistic Pillow", Jefferson Airplane, 1967

327. "Tidal", Fiona Apple, 1996

326. "The Woods", Sleater-Kinney, 2005

325. "The Sidewinder", Lee Morgan, 1964

324. "All Mod Cons", The Jam , 1978

323. "Franz Ferdinand", Franz Ferdinand, 2004

322. "This Nation's Saving Grace", The Fall, 1985

321. "Chicago Transit Authority", Chicago, 1969

I am of the opinion that Chicago was the most talented group of individuals ever to form a rock band and that, if they wrote better songs, they would dominate this list like The Beatles. Their absurdly ambitious debut survives mediocre songwriting by virtue of the breathtaking skill of musicians like Terry Kath and Walter Parazaider.

320. "Aenima", Tool, 1996

319. "Our Endless Numbered Days", Iron and Wine, 2004

318. "Vs.", Pearl Jam, 1993

317. "The Coral", The Coral, 2002

316. "Parallel Lines", Blondie, 1978

315. "On the Beach", Neil Young, 1974

314. "Tracy Chapman", Tracy Chapman, 1988

313. "Liquid Swords", GZA, 1995

312. "Copper Blue", Sugar, 1992

311. "Twin Cinema", The New Pornographers, 1992

310. "Little Creatures", Talking Heads, 1985

309. "Imperial Bedroom",
     Elvis Costello and The Attractions, 1982

308. "All Things Must Pass", George Harrison, 1970

307. "Music from Big Pink", The Band, 1967

306. "In a Silent Way", Miles Davis, 1969

305. "Silver Apples", Silver Apples, 1968

304. "The Midnight Organ Fight", Frightened Rabbit, 2008

303. "Deadringer", RJD2, 2002

302. "ATLiens", OutKast, 1996

301. "Neon Golden", The Notwist, 2002

> *This list has a complicated relationship with Germany. The Monks were Americans stationed there. Nico and Me'shell Ndegeocello were born there, but recorded primarily in the US. Can were formed there, but hired a Japanese singer. Neu!, Kraftwerk, and The Notwist seem to be the purest German bands on the list.*

HIDDEN GEMS

. . . . .

As mentioned in prior essays, many of these 1,000 albums are staples on public and private music lists. Here are ten albums in my top 500 (including three in the pages to come) that don't enjoy the same popular consensus. Each of these albums sits outside the top 10,000 on besteveralbums.com's overall list, which typically means that fewer than 20 users have found room for them on a list of their favorites albums of a year, decade, or all time. While I'll argue that each one deserves more recognition, there's a certain kinship a listener feels with an album that may not grab the world's attention, but speaks directly to them. These albums are my kin.

"OCCASIONAL RAIN",
Terry Callier, 1972
BEA RANK: 11,375   MY RANK: 62

In a just world, Terry Callier would have been a household name for the past 50 years, packing concert halls rather than coffee shops and swapping album sales numbers with Eagles or Jackson Browne. As a poet, a singer, and an arranger of parts for guest musicians of all stripes, Callier had few peers, and those skills are most pronounced on "Occasional Rain". "Ordinary Joe" is folk with a bite. "Do You Finally Need a Friend" is an ascent to heaven with a choir of angels. "Blues for Marcus" is Ella's scat over Nick Drake's cello. And "Lean On Me" is an epic with two parts heart and one part muscle.

"BRIGHT FLIGHT",
Silver Jews, 2001
BEA RANK: 14,479   MY RANK: 235

The lack of praise for this one may come from the absence of Stephen Malkmus, but Silver Jews are David Berman's project and he delivers better songs here than on any of the group's other records. He's more poet than singer, but the production is rich and warm and songs like "I Remember Me" and "Tennessee" won't soon escape your head.

"WORKOUT",
Hank Mobley, 1961
BEA RANK: 21,544   MY RANK: 330

Aptly titled, the sax man and his quintet keep heartrates up throughout "Workout". The opening title track is a stunning display of skill and pace, never letting up over ten frantic minutes. The album's lack of popular consensus probably speaks more to the 57 years that have elapsed since its recording than to its quality. Fans and critics tend to prefer Mobley's "Soul Station", but I don't hear the same intensity on that one.

"SHRIEK",
Wye Oak, 2014
BEA RANK: 18,427   MY RANK: 397

One thing about which I agree with fans and critics is that this album doesn't live up to the greatness of its murky predecessor, "Civilian". That said, a Wye Oak with less feedback and more melody shifts the focus from Andy Stack's drums to Jenn Wasner's voice, an equally imposing weapon. "Schools of Eyes" and "Paradise" alone are worth the price of admission.

"WISH SOMEONE
WOULD CARE",
Wye Oak, 2014
BEA RANK: 55,808   MY RANK: 400

This one's a complete unknown on besterveralbums, not appearing in so much as one user's 100 favorite albums of the 1960s. Give it one listen and you'll wonder why. Her voice is as big as Etta's and nearly rivals Aretha's and she pours 100% of herself into this debut album. The sublime title track blows the rest of the record away, but her covers of classics "Time is on My Side" and "I Need You So" prove the chops that earned Thomas the title "Soul Queen of New Orleans".

"THE ORDER OF TIME",
Valerie June, 2017
BEA RANK: 14,827   MY RANK: 407

Ironically, this album's failure to land in BEA's top 10,000 probably has as much to do with the order of time than with critical reception. June's brand of Southern Americana is as wholly unique as her rich, if reedy, voice. She shepherds the listener through a range of emotions before closing with a down-home singalong, "Got Soul".

"NEW VIEW",
Eleanor Friedberger, 2016
BEA RANK: 23,010   MY RANK: 408

Those of us who rank music often demand more than pleasant melodies before calling an album great. We want a record to break new ground or to sound like nothing we've heard before. With The Fiery Furnaces, Eleanor Friedberger did these things, pushing every envelope and refusing to relent to pop sensibility. On her third solo album, she put all experiments aside and made a straightforward folk-pop album with eleven songs worthy of praise without dissection.

"QUALITY",
Talib Kweli, 2002
BEA RANK: 13,949   MY RANK: 428

I struggle to understand why this socially conscious hip-hop record doesn't get more love. Sure, there's some filler ("Gun Music" is pretty awful), but I dare you to find a funnier intro than "Keynote Speaker", a better adrenaline surge than "Rush", or a better use of a sample than Nina Simone's "Sinnerman" in "Get By".

"TRONIC",
Black Milk, 2008
BEA RANK: 26,017   MY RANK: 430

On "Bounce", Detroit rapper Black Milk declares himself the "best artist not on your radio play", and there seems to be evidence to support that claim. A skilled rapper, lyricist, and drummer, it's the production, with samples that feel like they're coming live from the studio, that separates Black Milk from the competition. While besteveralbums users can't find room for one of his albums in the top 25,000, I've got two in my top 850, as the jazzy "No Poison, No Paradise" nearly equals this one.

"MERCY, MERCY, MERCY!",
Cannonball Adderley, 1966
BEA RANK: 13,949   MY RANK: 431

The first two tracks on "Mercy, Mercy, Mercy!" are called "Fun" and "Games", appropriate epithets for the output of a man willing to stretch the truth to help a friend. Ostensibly a live album recorded at Club DeLisa in Chicago, this one was actually recorded in a Hollywood studio with a staged audience. The alto saxophonist agreed to advertise the album as a live one as a favor for a friend who owned the club and wanted the publicity. Pieces like the sublime title track and the wonderful "Sticks" show up for the first time on a Cannonball Adderley record, so this is no live repackaging of old favorites that would be ineligible for this list. Good thing, because it's a gem.

ALBUMS
300-201

• • • • •

42 of these next 100 records are by bands who only show up once on the list, these true masterpieces standing out among their collections. These pages are full of Voodoo and Melodrama. England shakes, warm jets flow, somebody's nut goes flake, and hell hath no fury like these next hundred albums.

300. "Five Leaves Left", Nick Drake, 1969

> *My affection for Nick Drake may be inversely related to the adoration of critics and most fans, as I want so much more out of the acclaimed "Pink Moon" and find so much more in the ignored "Bryter Later". We agree that sparse, delicate debut "Five Leaves Left" falls in between.*

299. "Strictly Business", EPMD, 1988

298. "Boys and Girls", Alabama Shakes, 2012

297. "The Glow, Pt. 2", The Microphones, 2001

296. "Histoire de Melody Nelson", Serge Gainsbourg, 1971

295. "In it for the Money", Supergrass, 1997

294. "Never Mind the Bollocks Here's the Sex Pistols",
     Sex Pistols , 1977

293. "Neon Bible", Arcade Fire, 2007

292. "The Score", Fugees, 1996

291. "Fire of Love", The Gun Club, 1981

290. "Something Else by the Kinks", The Kinks, 1967

289. "Help!", The Beatles, 1965

288. "One Beat", Sleater-Kinney, 2002

> *My second-favorite of six Sleater-Kinney albums on the list, "One Beat" is perhaps the most aware and mature document in the wake of the September 11 attacks. It's almost as if the band's socially conscience punk was waiting for the world to be reduced to rubble from which they could rebuild it.*

287. "Moon Safari", Air, 1998

286. "Full Moon Fever", Tom Petty, 1989

285. "The Clash", The Clash, 1977

284. "The Decline of British Sea Power",
     British Sea Power, 2003

283. "The Sermon", Jimmy Smith, 1958

282. "In Ear Park", Department of Eagles, 2008

281. "Are We There", Sharon Van Etten, 2014

280. "Tapestry", Carole King, 1971

279. "Houses of the Holy", Led Zeppelin, 1973

278. "Thirteen Tales from Urban Bohemia",
The Dandy Warhols, 2000

277. "Dusty in Memphis", Dusty Springfield, 1969

276. "Here Come the Warm Jets", Brian Eno, 1974

275. "Loaded", The Velvet Underground, 1970

274. "Mellon Collie and the Infinite Sadness",
The Smashing Pumpkins, 1995

The double album is always a risk, especially when it runs over two hours. "Mellon Collie and the Infinite Sadness" definitely contains some filler, but its high points are inextricable from many of the high points of my teenage years, so it cracks the top 300 despite its excess.

273. "Stand!", Sly & the Family Stone, 1969

272. "Ys", Joanna Newsom, 2006

271. "Carrie & Lowell", Sufjan Stevens, 2015

270. "Journey in Satchidananda", Alice Coltrane, 1971

269. "Electric Warrior", T. Rex, 1971

268. "Hadestown", Anais Mitchell, 2010

267. "Nowhere", Ride, 1990

266. "Break it Yourself", Andrew Bird, 2012

265. "Merriweather Post Pavilion", Animal Collective , 2009

264. "Inspiration Information 3",
Mulatu Astatke & The Heliocentrics, 2009

263. "Gris-Gris", Dr. John, 1968

262. "I Love You, Honeybear", Father John Misty, 2015

261. "Moanin'", Art Blakey and the Jazz Messengers, 1958

> *Art Blakey and The Jazz Messengers score two albums on the list and an additional honorable mention, but their catalog is far deeper than that, as "A Night in Tunisia", "Indestructible", and "Buhaina's Delight" were all strong contenders.*

260. "Graceland", Paul Simon, 1986

259. "Being There", Wilco, 1996

258. "You Forgot it in People", Broken Social Scene, 2002

257. "In Rainbows", Radiohead, 2007

256. "Blue Lines", Massive Attack, 1991

255. "Lonerism", Tame Impala, 2012

254. "Voodoo", D'Angelo, 2000

253. "Emergency & I", The Dismemberment Plan, 1999

252. "Gulag Orkestar", Beirut, 2006

251. "Meddle", Pink Floyd, 1971

250. "Wild is the Wind", Nina Simone, 1966

249. "Picaresque", The Decemberists, 2005

248. "The College Dropout", Kanye West, 2004

247. "Sometimes I Sit and Think; Sometimes I Just Sit", Courtney Barnett, 2015

246. "Hail to the Thief", Radiohead, 2003

245. "John Lennon/Plastic Ono Band", John Lennon, 1970

244. "Melodrama", Lorde, 2017

> *A radio-friendly pop album released in the last year of the study might feel out of place in this stratosphere of the list, but look a little deeper and you'll find one of the most inspired and uplifting breakup albums recorded in any era.*

243. "Teen Dream", Beach House, 2010

242. "Parsley, Sage, Rosemary, & Thyme", Simon & Garfunkel, 1966

241. "The Infamous", Mobb Deep, 1995

240. "At Last!", Etta James, 1960

239. "Portishead", Portishead, 1997

238. "Bright Flight", Silver Jews, 2001

237. "Low", David Bowie, 1977

236. "In Utero", Nirvana, 1993

235. "Bringing It All Back Home", Bob Dylan, 1965

234. "Let's Stay Together", Al Green, 1972

233. "The Milk-Eyed Mender", Joanna Newsom, 2004

232. "The Argument", Fugazi, 2001

231. "Whatever People Say I Am, That's What I'm Not", Arctic Monkeys, 2006

230. "Phrenology", The Roots, 2002

229. "Be", Common, 2005

228. "Disreali Gears", Cream, 1967

227. "Here's Little Richard", Little Richard, 1957

> *With bonus points for historical context, it wouldn't be unreasonable to put this in the top 50. On the merits of the songs and recording quality alone, it's a top 250 album, better than any other non-jazz album released prior to 1963. A landmark achievement.*

226. "Central Reservation", Beth Orton, 1999

225. "Either/Or", Elliott Smith, 1997

224. "Lady Soul", Aretha Franklin, 1968

223. "The Allman Brothers Band", The Allman Brothers Band, 1969

222. "Hospice", The Antlers, 2009

221. "Stories from the City, Stories from the Sea", PJ Harvey, 2000

220. "Germ Free Adolescents", X-Ray Spex, 1978

219. "How I Got Over", The Roots, 2010

218. "I'm Wide Awake, It's Morning", Bright Eyes, 2005

217. "Paranoid", Black Sabbath, 1970

216. "The ArchAndroid (Suites II and III)", Janelle Monae, 2010

215. "Hell Hath No Fury", Clipse, 2006

214. "The Violent Femmes", The Violent Femmes, 1983

213. "The Gilded Palace of Sin",
     The Flying Burrito Brothers, 1969

212. "Ogden's Nut Gone Flake", Small Faces, 1968

211. "Actor", St. Vincent, 2009

210. "Let England Shake", PJ Harvey, 2011

209. "Sister", Sonic Youth, 1987

208. "Pretzel Logic", Steely Dan, 1974

207. "Ten", Pearl Jam, 1991

206. "The Greatest", Cat Power, 2006

205. "You Are Free", Cat Power, 2003

> *Many artists land multiple albums in close proximity to each other at some point on this list, but only The Beatles, The National, and Cat Power score back-to-back albums. These two come from very different places but are almost indistinguishably excellent.*

204. "Channel Orange", Frank Ocean, 2012

203. "Under the Pink", Tori Amos, 1994

202. "Everybody Knows This is Nowhere",
     Neil Young & Crazy Horse, 1969

201. "Source Tags and Codes", ...And You Will Know Us By
     the Trail of Dead, 2002

*When I look back on this list in a few years, this may
be the one album I regret not moving up a hundred
spots or more. Its unapologetic fury may not match
any of the templates established by the albums ahead
of it, but it carves out a perfection all its own.*

WHO DOMINATES THIS LIST?
ARTISTS WHO APPEAR AT LEAST THREE TIMES

● ● ● ● ●

Below are the artists with three or more entries among my top 1,000 albums, ranked by the point system described in the "Can Today's Music Compete with the Classics?" essay above:

RANK	ARTIST	POINTS	#
1	The Beatles	37,586	10
2	Bob Dylan	32,223	11
3	Radiohead	26,325	7
4	Led Zeppelin	23,534	6
5	Miles Davis	23,098	9
6	R.E.M.	22,661	9
7	The Rolling Stones	19,370	5
8	Velvet Underground	16,731	4
9	David Bowie	16,417	6
10	Neil Young	16,100	6
11	Stevie Wonder	16,064	5

RANK	ARTIST	POINTS	#
12	OutKast	15,517	5
13	Blur	15,171	5
14	Talking Heads	15,067	5
15	Pink Floyd	13,929	5
16	Sonic Youth	13,865	6
17	Sleater-Kinney	13,694	6
18	Pavement	13,387	3
19	Wilco	13,199	4
20	Kendrick Lamar	13,116	4
21	Beck	12,703	6
22	Bruce Springsteen	12,568	5
23	Kanye West	12,495	3
24	Arcade Fire	12,429	3
25	The Decemberists	12,362	4
26	Elton John	11,682	4
27	Charles Mingus	11,533	4
28	The Roots	11,529	3
29	A Tribe Called Quest	11,496	4
30	Van Morrison	11,411	5
31	Tom Waits	11,275	4
32	PJ Harvey	11,123	5
33	Andrew Bird	10,945	4

RANK	ARTIST	POINTS	#
34	The Jimi Hendrix Experience	10,910	3
35	Sufjan Stevens	10,861	3
36	Björk	10,685	3
37	Belle & Sebastian	10,588	4
38	The Smiths	10,561	4
39	Steely Dan	10,209	4
40	Elvis Costello	10,123	3
41	Joanna Newsom	10,016	3
42	The Stooges	9,860	3
43	Modest Mouse	9,844	3
44	Simon & Garfunkel	9,730	3
45	John Coltrane	9,630	3
46	Big Star	9,550	3
47	Public Enemy	9,534	3
48	Portishead	9,514	3
49	Pixies	9,473	3
50	The Smashing Pumpkins	9,413	3
51	Joni Mitchell	9,370	5
52	Fiona Apple	9,255	3
53	Nick Drake	9,160	3
54	King Crimson	8,909	4
55	Elliott Smith	8,818	3

RANK	ARTIST	POINTS	#
56	The White Stripes	8,778	3
57	The Allman Brothers Band	8,647	3
58	Nirvana	8,543	3
59	Nick Cave & Bad Seeds	8,165	4
60	Silver Jews	8,141	3
61	Eminem	8,042	3
62	The Police	7,856	3
63	Sigur Rós	7,807	3
64	Cocteau Twins	7,748	3
65	The Shins	7,744	3
66	Of Montreal	7,645	3
67	Grizzly Bear	7,418	3
68	LCD Soundsystem	7,407	3
69	Kate Bush	7,291	3
70	The New Pornographers	7,252	3
71	The Kinks	7,087	3
72	Leonard Cohen	6,903	3
73	Black Sabbath	6,714	3
74	Al Green	6,684	3
75	Beth Orton	6,390	3
76	Iron and Wine	6,271	3
77	Paul Simon	5,990	3

RANK	ARTIST	POINTS	#
78	Yo La Tengo	5,985	3
79	The Byrds	5,856	3
80	Roxy Music	5,758	4
81	Bonnie "Prince" Billy	5,756	3
82	Spoon	5,629	3
83	Can	5,415	3
84	Beastie Boys	5,409	3
85	Creedence Clearwater Revival	5,382	3
86	Okkervil River	5,300	3
87	Metallica	5,250	4
88	Gorillaz	4,749	3
89	Laura Marling	2,854	3
90	Ben Folds Five	2,327	3

ALBUMS
200-101

● ● ● ● ●

The Beatles and Led Zeppelin each land two albums here, but they're both far from done. The Stooges, Talking Heads, and Flaming Lips each land their two best albums in this section, as do David Bowie, Blur, Jay-Z, and The National. Two of the great modern country albums rub elbows with eleven hip-hop classics.

200. "Music of My Mind", Stevie Wonder, 1972

Lost between Little Stevie's sugar-coated Motown singles and the mid-'70s Grammy fodder is grownup Stevie's first self-authored masterpiece, a gumbo of pop, funk, and hard-charging R&B that changed the rules for songwriters of the '70s.

199. "Amnesiac", Radiohead, 2001

198. "Black Monk Time", The Monks, 1966

197. "I Am a Bird Now", Antony and the Johnsons, 2005

196. "White Light/White Heat",
      The Velvet Underground, 1968

195. "Bee Thousand", Guided by Voices, 1994

194. "Tim", The Replacements, 1985

193. "Elastica", Elastica, 1995

192. "A Crow Looked At Me", Mount Eerie, 2017

Phil Elverum shows up twice on the list with more rich and textured music as The Microphones, but this rumination on the death of his wife and his experience raising their infant daughter alone is his most moving work.

191. "The Low End Theory", A Tribe Called Quest, 1991

190. "Since I Left You", The Avalanches, 2000

189. "Everything Must Go", Manic Street Preachers, 1996

188. "Odelay", Beck, 1996

187. "Up in Flames", Caribou (as Manitoba), 2003

186. "Mezzanine", Massive Attack, 1998

185. "Moondance", Van Morrison, 1970

184. "Hot Rats", Frank Zappa, 1969

183. "Permutation", Amon Tobin, 1998

182. "Summer Teeth", Wilco, 1999

181. "New Day Rising", Hüsker Dü, 1985

180. "Otis Blue/Otis Redding Sings Soul",
     Otis Redding, 1965

179. "New Adventures in H-Fi", R.E.M., 1996

178. "Bridge Over Troubled Water",
     Simon & Garfunkel, 1970

177. "Weezer" (Blue), Weezer, 1994

176. "Boxer", The National, 2007

175. "High Violet", The National, 2010

174. "The Navigator", Hurray for the Riff Raff, 2017

173. "I Do Not Want What I Haven't Got",
     Sinéad O'Connor, 1990

> *When I first started exploring the music of the past in the late '90s, 1990 was the one year from which I couldn't find anything I liked. As it turns out, I didn't even have to search beyond (possibly) my extended family to find the year's most daringly defiant and deftly crafted album.*

172. "White Blood Cells", The White Stripes, 2001

171. "The Blueprint", Jay-Z, 2001

170. "Purple Rain", Prince, 1984

169. "Black Sheep Boy", Okkervil River, 2005

168. "Rubber Soul", The Beatles, 1965

167. "Reasonable Doubt", Jay-Z, 1996

166. "Skylarking", XTC, 1986

165. "Dig Me Out", Sleater-Kinney, 1997

164. "Slanted and Enchanted", Pavement, 1992

163. "Fever to Tell", Yeah Yeah Yeahs, 2003

162. "Are You Experienced?",
     The Jimi Hendrix Experience, 1967

161. "Bitte Orca", Dirty Projectors, 2009

160. "Brothers", The Black Keys, 2010

159. "xx", The xx, 2009

158. "A Sailor's Guide to Earth", Sturgill Simpson, 2016

> *I only identify 15 of these 1,000 albums as country, a genre that tends not to speak to me, but "A Sailor's Guide to Earth", Simpson's brilliant musical letter to his newborn son, would stand out in any genre.*

157. "(What's the Story) Morning Glory", Oasis, 1995

156. "Buffalo Springfield Again", Buffalo Springfield, 1967

155. "Mingus Ah Um", Charles Mingus, 1959

154. "Night Falls Over Kortedala", Jens Lekman, 2007

153. "Internal Wrangler", Clinic, 2000

152. "Fun House", The Stooges, 1970

151. "Deserter's Songs", Mercury Rev, 1998

150. "Led Zeppelin II", Led Zeppelin, 1969

149. "The Marshall Mathers LP", Eminem, 2000

148. "Things Fall Apart", The Roots, 1999

147. "The Chronic", Dr. Dre, 1992

146. "Let it Be", The Beatles, 1970

145. "The Joshua Tree", U2, 1987

144. "Urban Hymns", The Verve, 1997

143. "Modern Life is Rubbish", Blur, 1993

142. "Bitches Brew", Miles Davis, 1970

141. "Ready to Die", The Notorious B.I.G., 1994

140. "Treasure", Cocteau Twins, 1984

139. "Yoshimi Battles the Pink Robots", The Flaming Lips, 2002

Few albums from the 21st century qualify as canon, but "Yoshimi", most notably "Do You Realize??" and "Fight Test", pass the popular appeal and critical credibility tests like few other records from that time. We didn't know 2002 needed an album about a little girl fighting robots, but we're better off for having gotten one.

138. "Parklife", Blur, 1994

137. "Goodbye Yellow Brick Road", Elton John, 1973

136. "The Miseducation of Lauryn Hill", Lauryn Hill, 1998

135. "Moby Grape", Moby Grape, 1967

134. "Odessey and Oracle", The Zombies, 1968

133. "The Soft Bulletin", The Flaming Lips, 1999

132. "Van Lear Rose", Loretta Lynn, 2004

131. "The Suburbs", Arcade Fire, 2010

130. "This Year's Model", Elvis Costello, 1978

129. "Crosby, Stills, & Nash", Crosby, Stills, & Nash, 1969

128. "Murmur", R.E.M., 1983

127. "The Moon and Antarctica", Modest Mouse, 2000

126. "Tigermilk", Belle & Sebastian, 1996

125. "Synchronicity", The Police, 1983

124. "The Wild, The Innocent, & The E Street Shuffle", Bruce Springsteen, 1973

> *Springsteen's later work tackled bigger issues lyrically and earned broader appeal, but his composition skills were never better showcased than on his rollicking second album, "The Wild, The Innocent, & The E Street Shuffle".*

123. "The Modern Lovers", The Modern Lovers, 1976

122. "The King is Dead", The Decemberists, 2011

121. "For Your Pleasure", Roxy Music, 1973

120. "Blood on the Tracks", Bob Dylan, 1975

119. "Remain in Light", Talking Heads, 1980

118. "Tea for the Tillerman", Cat Stevens, 1970

117. "The Doors", The Doors, 1967

116. "The Rise and Fall of Ziggy Stardust and the Spiders from Mars", David Bowie, 1972

115. "For Emma, Forever Ago", Bon Iver, 2007

114. "Late Registration", Kanye West, 2005

113. "What's Going On?", Marvin Gaye, 1971

112. "Raw Power", The Stooges, 1973

111. "Who's Next", The Who, 1971

110. "Beggars Banquet", The Rolling Stones, 1968

109. "Chutes Too Narrow", The Shins, 2003

108. "Closer", Joy Division, 1980

107. "Fear of a Black Planet", Public Enemy, 1990

106. "More Songs About Buildings and Food",
     Talking Heads, 1978

105. (Led Zeppelin IV), Led Zeppelin, 1971

104. "Hunky Dory", David Bowie, 1971

103. "Surfer Rosa", Pixies, 1988

102. "Aja", Steely Dan, 1977

> *Steely Dan's finely crafted brand of jazz-rock tends to garner as much scorn as praise, but the seven tracks on "Aja" could not have been written and played by anyone but the supremely talented Walter Becker and Donald Fagen.*

101. "The Songs of Leonard Cohen", Leonard Cohen, 1968

FRIENDS AND FAMILY

● ● ● ● ●

The prior interlude identified the artists who show up most frequently and with the highest ranked albums. What that chart misses are the myriad connections between the 626 different artists whose albums make the list. If I had defined "artist" as an individual releasing a solo album or contributing to a band's effort, would that list have been much different? What if I had gone in the other direction, giving bands credit for the solo contributions of their members?

Let's take a look at some "music families"- musicians who played with multiple bands or under multiple monikers or collaborated with other musicians on album-length projects. The Beatles, for instance, landed ten albums and scored a list-high 37,586 points. Add one album each from John Lennon, George Harrison, and Paul McCartney & Wings, and the Fab Four are up to 13 albums and 44,524 points.

Two other groups show up on the list as a unit and as three separate members: The New Pornographers, if combined with albums by Destroyer, Neko Case (solo and as part of Case/Lang/Viers), and AC Newman, would finish higher than Pavement, Wilco, and Kendrick Lamar in rank points. And the Wu-Tang Clan lands their debut in the top fifty, with members GZA, Raekwon, and Ghostface Killah (twice) represented as well. Their collective score would top A Tribe Called Quest, Van Morrison, and Tom Waits.

All four Velvet Underground albums are in the top 300, while John Cale and Lou Reed each contribute a solo album. If we count Nico, the group that put out my 13th favorite album of all time has eight albums on the list and more points than The Rolling Stones.

Even more impressive, members of the Miles Davis Quintet, including John Coltrane and Cannonball Adderley, score 40,210 points. That's better than The Beatles, excluding their members' solo efforts.

Lauryn Hill and Wyclef Jean join the Fugees to score more points than Nirvana. Adding Robert Plant's collaboration with Alison Krauss to Led Zeppelin's score would be almost enough for Zeppelin to reach Radiohead's perch in third place.

If we shift our focus from band members who went solo to musicians who played in several groups, Damon Albarn is our new hero. Part of five albums on the list by Blur, three by Gorillaz, and one as a solo artist, Albarn scores 19,972 points over nine records. That's top-ten territory.

Eric Clapton makes the list as a solo artist and as part of Cream (twice), Derek & the Dominos, and Blind Faith. His combined rank score sits between PJ Harvey and Andrew Bird.

Daniel Dumile recorded as MF Doom and Viktor Vaughn, while scoring most of his points as half of Madvillain. Madvillain collaborator Madlib teamed up with Freddie Gibbs for yet another entry. Will Oldham recorded as both Bonnie "Prince" Billy and Palace Music, totaling more points than Black Sabbath.

Bob Mould scored exactly one album each as part of Hüsker Dü, the frontman of Sugar, and a solo singer/songwriter. Paul Simon lands three albums on his own after parting with Art Garfunkel, totaling more points than Stevie Wonder.

Finally, the list includes David Byrne collaborations, 31 years apart, with Brian Eno and St. Vincent. Eno makes the list as a member of Roxy Music (though he appears on just one of their four entries) and twice as a solo artist (and I'd need a team of interns to try to count all the albums Eno produced or contributed to). St. Vincent adds two of her own albums, both in the top 400. And, of course, Byrne's Talking Heads show up five times on the list. David Byrne's total rank score of 18,347 would top David Bowie and Neil Young, though not if we add Neil's points as a member of Buffalo Springfield and Crosby, Stills, Nash, & Young.

In addition to music families, there are a few actual family connections on this list. John Coltrane's three albums complement one by his wife Alice and two by their grandnephew, Steven Ellison, who records as Flying Lotus. Father and son Tim and Jeff Buckley each hold one spot. And Rufus Wainwright contributes two albums while his mother, Kate McGarricle, was part of the duo responsible for album #884.

My definition of "artist" may be unfair to Neko Case, David Byrne, and John Lennon, who charted the top album by a former Beatle, giving him 41,003 total rank points, more than anyone else. Conversely, expanding "artist" to "family" gives the Miles Davis Quartet an even greater claim to greatness.

ALBUMS 100-26

● ● ● ● ●

Every album from the start of this book to number 101 is fantastic and comes highly recommended. Perhaps the hardest part of this exercise was drawing this final line- deciding which 100 albums are my all-time favorites. The 1960s, 70s, and 90s each land 20 to 22 albums in the top 100, with 16 more from the 2000s, 11 from the '80s, eight from the 2010s, and three more from the eligible portion of the '50s.

100. "The Psychedelic Sounds of the 13th Floor Elevators", 13th Floor Elevators, 1966

99. "Sea Change", Beck, 2002

> *Beck has recorded a little of everything, but he never shone brighter than on his breakup album. I have very few breakups in my past, but the breakup album that resonated most deeply with me is cathartic to this day, helping to soften Ends of the Road of many types.*

98. "I Can Hear the Heart Beating as One", Yo La Tengo, 1997

97. "My Woman", Angel Olsen, 2016

96. "Thriller", Michael Jackson, 1982

95. "Pink Flag", Wire, 1977

94. "#1 Record", Big Star, 1972

93. "Hounds of Love", Kate Bush, 1985

92. "Paul's Boutique", The Beastie Boys, 1989

91. "Reckoning", R.E.M., 1984

90. "Astral Weeks", Van Morrison, 1968

89. "Tumbleweed Connection", Elton John, 1970

88. "When the Pawn Hits the Conflicts He Thinks Like a King What He Knows Throws the Blows When He Goes to the Fight and He'll Win the Whole Thing 'Fore He Enters the Ring There's No Body to Batter When Your Mind is Your Might So When You Go Solo, You Hold Your Own Hand and Remember That Depth Is the Greatest of Heights and If You Know Where You Stand, Then You Know Where to Land and If You Fall It Won't Matter, Cuz You'll Know That You're Right", Fiona Apple, 1999

> *The title may come off a bit pretentious, but its volume can scarcely contain the talent and wisdom embodied by the 22-year-old challenged to build on her Pitchfork-darling-meets-late-night-MTV debut.*

87. "Wowee Zowee", Pavement, 1995

86. "Ramones", Ramones, 1976

85. "Is This It?", The Strokes, 2001

84. "Pretenders", Pretenders, 1980

83. "Elephant", The White Stripes, 2003

82. "Forever Changes", Love, 1967

81. "Yankee Hotel Foxtrot", Wilco, 2002

80. "Blue Train", John Coltrane, 1957

79. "Horses", Patti Smith, 1975

78. "The Crane Wife", The Decemberists, 2006

> *The Decemberists are one of nine bands with albums in the top 100 who routinely employ both male and female singers. This is true of 20 of the top 200 albums, but just 46 of the remaining 800.*

77. "Back to Black", Amy Winehouse, 2006

76. "Halcyon Digest", Deerhunter, 2010

75. "Dummy", Portishead, 1994

74. "The Freewheelin' Bob Dylan", Bob Dylan, 1963

73. "Siamese Dream", The Smashing Pumpkins, 1993

72. "The Cars", The Cars, 1978

71. "Rain Dogs", Tom Waits, 1985

70. "Pearl", Janis Joplin, 1971

69. "Hot Buttered Soul", Isaac Hayes, 1969

68. "Exile in Guyville", Liz Phair, 1993

67. "Revolver", The Beatles, 1966

66. "Sound of Silver", LCD Soundsystem, 2007

65. "The Velvet Underground",
    The Velvet Underground, 1969

64. "Sticky Fingers", The Rolling Stones, 1971

63. "Homogenic", Björk, 1997

62. "Occasional Rain", Terry Callier, 1972

61. "Illmatic", Nas, 1994

60. "Automatic for the People", R.E.M., 1992

59. "The Dark Side of the Moon", Pink Floyd, 1973

58. "Fleet Foxes", Fleet Foxes, 2008

57. "My Beautiful Dark Twisted Fantasy", Kanye West, 2010

56. "Bryter Layter", Nick Drake, 1970

55. "Teens of Denial", Car Seat Headrest, 2016

54. "Let it Be", The Replacements, 1984

> *This top 1000 contains two albums each called "Desire", "Giant Steps", "Los Angeles", "Smile", and "Let it Be". Expanding the post-hardcore vocabulary to express teen angst with heart, this is the sloppiest, most wonderful record of them all.*

53. "Veckatimest", Grizzly Bear, 2009

52. "Innervisions", Stevie Wonder, 1973

51. "The Black Saint and the Sinner Lady",
    Charles Mingus, 1963

> *More than half of the 45 albums on this list that I identify as jazz were released between 1957 and 1962. "Black Saint and the Sinner Lady" is the highest-ranking jazz album released after '62.*

50. "The Bends", Radiohead, 1995

49. "Blonde on Blonde", Bob Dylan, 1966

48. "Grace", Jeff Buckley, 1994

47. "Layla and Other Assorted Love Songs",
    Derek & The Dominos, 1970

46. "Ritual de lo Habitual", Jane's Addiction, 1990

45. "London Calling", The Clash, 1979

44. "In the Court of the Crimson King", King Crimson, 1969

43. "Enter the Wu-Tang (36 Chambers)",
    Wu-Tang Clan, 1993

42. "To Pimp a Butterfly", Kendrick Lamar, 2015

41. "Civilian", Wye Oak, 2011

40. "Kid A", Radiohead, 2000

39. "Illinoise", Sufjan Stevens, 2005

38. "Muchacho", Phosphorescent, 2013

37. "Led Zeppelin", Led Zeppelin, 1969

36. "If You're Feeling Sinister", Belle & Sebastian, 1996

35. "I Never Loved a Man (the Way I Love You)", Aretha Franklin, 1967

34. "The Beatles", The Beatles, 1968

33. "Aquemini", OutKast, 1998

32. "Physical Graffiti", Led Zeppelin, 1975

31. "Doolittle", Pixies, 1989

30. "Sgt. Pepper's Lonely Hearts Club Band", The Beatles, 1967

29. "Agaetis Byrjun", Sigur Rós, 1999

28. "Nevermind", Nirvana, 1991

27. "Rumours", Fleetwood Mac, 1977

26. "It Takes a Nation of Millions to Hold Us Back", Public Enemy, 1988

> *Of 92 hip-hop albums on this list, only three predate the release of "It Takes a Nation of Millions to Hold Us Back". This is the only '80s rap album in the top 90.*

ALBUMS 25-11

● ● ● ● ●

25. "I See a Darkness", Bonnie "Prince" Billy, 1999
    *A gloomy record that sometimes doesn't feel like music,
    this one somehow finds enough hooks to stick on your
    head for days despite its depressing overtones.*

24. "Hissing Fauna, Are You the Destroyer?",
    Of Montreal, 2007
    *Just another self-psychoanalysis joyride, this one's about
    as weird as it gets, musically and lyrically, but Kevin
    Barnes commits to his theme and delivers perfect song
    after perfect song.*

23. "Electric Ladyland", The Jimi Hendrix Experience, 1968
    *As audacious as anything in the rock canon, this is maybe
    the peak of late-'60s rock and roll. Two epics prove Jimi's
    technical superiority, but it peaks with a four-minute cover
    of a folk song.*

22. "Exile on Main Street", The Rolling Stones, 1972
    *By my count, this is not the Stones' best album, but it's the
    best 2nd-best album anyone's ever released. It explodes
    out of the gate and rarely lets up over 18 songs and 67
    minutes.*

21. "After the Gold Rush", Neil Young, 1970
    Nobody does Americana like this Canadian singer-songwriter. His second solo album adds occasional heavy guitar, but the best songs are incisive folk tunes and beautiful love songs.

20. "Madvillainy", Madvillain, 2004
    A genius by any name, Daniel Dumile peaks here as MF Doom. His raps weave classic R&B references in with tales of weed and halitosis, all over Madlib's kitchen-sink beats

19. "Daydream Nation", Sonic Youth, 1988
    The attitude that launched punk meets a legendary two-guitar attack, with song quality to match the dynamism of the performers.

18. "Crooked Rain Crooked Rain", Pavement, 1994
    The best American band of the '90s releases their defining statement between two other masterpieces, working in an uncharacteristic number of earworms.

17. "Let it Bleed", The Rolling Stones, 1969
    After half a decade chasing The Beatles, the Stones finally catch them here. It's dark and dangerous, opening and closing with landmark tracks that capture the sixties zeitgeist.

16. "Abbey Road", The Beatles, 1969
    The greatest band in history goes out at the top of its game. Side one is full of classic rock staples, while side two is a stunningly-produced ride through a fascinating world.

15. "In the Aeroplane Over the Sea",
    Neutral Milk Hotel, 1998
    More an immersive history lesson than a music record,
    Jeff Mangum's band used cacophony and unorthodox
    instruments to weave beautiful tales of love, death, and
    heartache.

14. "Loveless", My Bloody Valentine, 1991
    1991 changed everything, but it wasn't just "Nevermind".
    This is one of the great examples of texture as the defining
    characteristic of an album.

13. "The Velvet Underground and Nico",
    The Velvet Underground, 1967
    Perhaps the ultimate counterculture statement by the
    ultimate art-rock group. Andy Warhol introduced his
    nascent road show to a sultry chanteuse and his blender
    spit out an all-timer.

12. "Kind of Blue", Miles Davis, 1959
    The epitome of cool, this is the one jazz album that graces
    every fan's collection, and for good reason, as this is as
    easy on the ears as it is groundbreaking. Just one jazz
    album ranks higher.

11. "Stankonia", OutKast, 2000
    "Stankonia" is full of earworms rapped and sung and
    played by two of the smoothest, sharpest-tongued guys in
    the hip-hip industry- or any industry, for that matter.

THE TOP 10

• • • • •

10. "ARMCHAIR APOCRYPHA", ☐ Andrew Bird, 2007

Among the top ten (and probably the top 25), this is the album least likely to show up on another fan's favorite albums list. Aside from Bird's small label's limited ability to market the music (and the absence of guest spots by Rihanna, I guess), I'm not sure I understand why this isn't among anyone else's favorites.

Andrew Bird is one of the more literate singer-songwriters I've heard. His lyrics are as clever as Morrissey's and as perceptive as McCartney's. I imagine one could hand him any instrument and he'd quickly play it as fluently as he does his violin and his guitar, if not as sublimely as his whistle, which carries several songs on "Armchair Apocrypha". I can't think of another musician capable of both writing and playing such richly diverse songs as "Armchairs", "Cataracts", and the divine "Spare-Ohs".

9. "FUNERAL",
□ Arcade Fire, 2004

To praise the best rock album of the 21st century as "worthy" of classic rock radio would be antithetical to this whole exercise. Access to better recording equipment has broadened the musical palette, allowing more musicians to share their ideas in sonically pleasing ways. Still, so much rock-and-roll ground was covered so well between the mid-sixties and early seventies that many of those new ideas tend to show up on hip-hop records, electronica, and music that doesn't conform to one genre or another. As the traditional rock band goes, maybe there's just not much left to say.

Enter Arcade Fire, whose major-label debut is built around the rock formula, but with as many as 15 musicians playing at once and songs that explore the human psyche in the wake of the death of a loved one, something multiple band members had recently experienced. Each song builds in intensity until closer "In the Backseat" paralyzes the listener's nervous system.

80 "PET SOUNDS", □ The Beach Boys, 1966

No matter what seventeen meant to you, if you were ever seventeen, you can relate to "Pet Sounds". While I write those words with great reverence for the Beach Boys and their crowning achievement, they could be used to describe many lesser albums and other works of "art". This album, though, is so honest in its yearning, so genuine in its nostalgia that it succeeds without resorting to any of the tropes that underlie a typical piece of teen sentimentalia.

"Wouldn't It Be Nice" is painfully direct, delivering a message no reasonable adult would agree with (cohabitation would heal teenage wounds) in a way that transports every adult back to an earlier life he may or may not have even lived. Similarly, "I'm Waiting for the Day" requires no prerequisite heartbreak to deliver the listener back to an idyllic-but-troubled childhood. The arrangements are simple but perfect; the harmonies almost hokey but almost impossible not to sing along to. God only knows whether I'd care about music without this album.

7. □ "THE QUEEN IS DEAD", The Smiths, 1986

"It's so easy to laugh, it's so easy to hate. It takes strength to be gentle and kind." This piece of tender wisdom comes from an album whose themes range from begging for cash from "a flatulent pain in the ass" to feeling the soil flowing over one's near-deceased head to joking with Sweetness that she should be bludgeoned in her bed. The most subversive, underground, anti-pop band ever to sell a million albums (and they sold a million *singles*) were such a delightful contradiction, blessing us with classic after classic throughout a decade in which the most popular forms of expression were legwarmers and feathered hair.

From the opening salvo leading into the title track to the cleverness-melts-off-the-bone "Bigmouth Strikes Again" to the iconic "There Is a Light That Never Goes Out", this was the most perfect album recorded outside of North America until the one you'll read about on the last page of this book.

6 "MARQUEE MOON", TELEVISION, 1977

The only album in the top ten by a band not represented elsewhere in the top 1,000, Television were one of rock's greatest flashes-in-the-pan. While punk was defining itself by stripping out musicianship and pounding the same chord until it bled, Television embraced punk's attitude while building their sound around Tom Verlaine's and Richard Lloyd's guitar wizardry.

The Ramones told us all we could write and play two-minute pop songs about beating on the brat with a baseball bat. Television reminded us with opuses like "Marquee Moon" and "Friction" that it's best to leave the songwriting and musicianship to the professionals, but we can all be part of the party.

5. □ "GOOD KID, M.A.A.D. CITY", KENDRICK LAMAR, 2012

The best album of the current decade sounds nothing like anything else in this top ten. It's a triumph of storytelling and production- not devoid of melody, but evocative more in its stark honesty than its musicality. Barely 25 at the time of its release, Kendrick Lamar had already built enough renown that an autobiographical concept album was met with considerable hype.

To say "Good Kid, M.A.A.D. City" lived up to the hype would be a Compton-sized understatement. Bookended by Lamar's dad ranting about Kendrick not bringing home his goddamn Domino's and telling him that being true to his family, not killing a man, will make him a real man, the hour in between explores all the relationships and pressures that a good kid faces in a city that chews up good kids and leaves them dead of thirst in a swimming pool full of liquor.

4. "SOMETHIN' ELSE", □ Cannonball Adderley, 1958

I listened to a few hundred jazz albums in compiling this project, but I'm neither a musician nor a critic, so I can't intelligently tell you why Cannonball's "Somethin' Else" tops everything by Miles, 'Trane, and Mingus as my favorite jazz album.

I can, however, tell you that the note Cannonball plays beginning at 8:32 of the opening track, "Autumn Leaves", is perfection. In the seventies and eighties, I believe Congress passed legislation dictating that the last time a chorus was played in a song, the most prominent note/word in said chorus must be played/sung at least a half an octave higher than its counterparts earlier in the tune. Over the years, many a song has been soiled by this trick, which often breaks a singer away from her comfort zone in an attempt to knock us off our feet for a fleeting moment. Cannonball's alto sax owned that higher note and delivered it so perfectly that I wish it were the last such lift in music history.

3 "HIGHWAY 61 REVISITED", □ Bob Dylan, 1965

It's not just the poetry, which is vitriolic and wry and pleading and desperate in ways few other songwriters could pull off. It's the new template for a singer, proving that one need not have a trained- or even pleasant- voice to qualify as a rock star. Like few before or since, Bob Dylan opens his mouth and invites us to tour every cunning nook and sardonic cranny of his brain.

On "Highway 61 Revisited", The Hawks keep the tempo behind him, guitar solos are accents and epilogues, not showstoppers, and the harmonica reminds us that this budding rocker is the same guy who wrote protest songs in the key of Woody Guthrie earlier in the decade.

I'll argue below that two better albums have been made since this one, but if you told me no one has topped Highway 61, you might not be wrong.

2 "BLUE",
☐ Joni Mitchell, 1971

Throughout the 1970s, Joni Mitchell released nothing but fantastic albums, but "Blue" stands head and shoulders above the rest. Neither overambitious and overproduced nor safe and predictable, every note on this record is perfection.

Joni's vocal gymnastics, particularly on "All I Want" and "California", are every bit as impressive as Jimi's guitar or Miles's trumpet. "River" doubles as the best holiday song ever written and one of the great breakup songs. "My Old Man" is a paean to a lover and a generation that refused to be governed by prior generations' rules. I could drink a case of this one and still be on my feet, heading to the CD player to press Play again.

1. "OK COMPUTER", ☐ Radiohead, 1997

At besteveralbums.com, fans have overwhelmingly voted "OK Computer" the best album of all time, with over 300 different users naming it first on their personal lists. At rateyourmusic. com, "OK Computer" leads the pack by an even larger margin. In 2005, a British Channel 4 panel named it the best album ever. In 2006, Q Magazine did the same.

Publications run by older music fans tend to stick to a Beatles album at the top, but among the younger generation, this one sits on top more often than not. Why write a whole book culminating in an opinion that lines up so well with popular opinion?

Because all these people are right.

We could talk about the groundbreaking injection of technology into the classic guitar/bass/ drums lineup or the timely paranoia the band captured so well, but to me, it's all about the sounds.

"OK Computer" is the best album ever because of the searing transitions between parts in "Paranoid Android". Because of the heavenly crescendo closing the hellscape of "Exit Music (for a Film)" and the how-did-he-do-that harmonies in "Let Down". It's the feeling in "Climbing Up the Walls" that he's really lurking around the next corner and the redemption in "Lucky" when we close our eyes and convince ourselves it's gonna be a glorious day.

THE NEAR MISSES
100 HONORABLE MENTIONS

• • • • •

A thousand is a lot of albums, but it's not enough to include all the great music recorded over 61 years. It wasn't easy leaving some of these next 100 albums (shown chronologically) off the list:

"Soulville", Ben Webster, 1957

"Milestones", Miles Davis, 1958

"Lady in Satin", Billie Holiday, 1958

"Jazz in Silhouette", Sun Ra & His Arkestra, 1959

"Berry is on Top", Chuck Berry, 1959

"Blues & Roots", Charles Mingus, 1960

"Focus", Stan Getz, 1961

"With the Beatles", The Beatles, 1963

"Free For All", Art Blakey & the Jazz Messengers, 1964

"Idle Moments", Grant Green, 1965

"I Put a Spell On You", Nina Simone, 1965

"Complete & Unbelievable: The Otis Redding Dictionary of Soul", Otis Redding, 1966

"Ascension", John Coltrane, 1966

"Chelsea Girl", Nico, 1967

"S.F. Sorrow", The Pretty Things, 1968

"Trout Mask Replica", Captain Beefheart & The Magic Band, 1969

"...to be Continued", Isaac Hayes, 1970

"Just Another Diamond Day", Vashti Bunyan, 1970

"The Man Who Sold the World", David Bowie, 1970

"12 Songs", Randy Newman, 1970

"Mulatu of Ethiopia", Mulatu Astatke, 1972

"Paris 1919", John Cale, 1973

"Veedon Fleece", Van Morrison, 1974

"A New World Record", Electric Light Orchestra, 1976

"Armed Forces", Elvis Costello and The Attractions, 1979

"Dirty Mind", Prince, 1980

"Ghost in the Machine", The Police, 1981

"The Dreaming", Kate Bush, 1982

"Hex Enduction Hour", The Fall, 1982

"High Land, Hard Rain", Aztec Camera, 1983

"Zen Arcade", Hüsker Dü, 1984

"Mantronix: The Album", Mantronix, 1985

"Fables of the Reconstruction", R.E.M., 1985

"Pleased to Meet Me", The Replacements, 1987

"Critical Beatdown", Ultramagnetic MCs", 1988

"Tender Prey", Nick Cave & The Bad Seeds, 1988

"Like a Prayer", Madonna, 1989

"New York", Lou Reed, 1989

"Pod", The Breeders, 1990

"Pills 'n' Thrills and Bellyaches", Happy Mondays, 1990

"Violator", Depeche Mode, 1990

"Let the Rhythm Hit 'Em", Eric B & Rakim, 1990

"Steady Diet of Nothing", Fugazi, 1991

"Rage Against the Machine", Rage Against the Machine, 1992

"A Storm in Heaven", The Verve, 1993

"Throwing Copper", Live, 1994

"Mellow Gold", Beck, 1994

"Diary", Sunny Day Real Estate, 1994

"Definitely Maybe", Oasis, 1994

"Washing Machine", Sonic Youth, 1995

"Wrecking Ball", Emmylou Harris, 1995

"Wu-Tang Forever", Wu-Tang Clan, 1997

"You've Come a Long Way, Baby", Fatboy Slim, 1998

"Black Star", Mos Def & Talib Kweli, 1998

"Moment of Truth", Gang Starr, 1998

"Ray of Light", Madonna, 1998

"Little Plastic Castle", Ani DiFranco, 1998

"Featuring 'Birds'", Quasi, 1998

"Mule Variations", Tom Waits, 1999

"Like Water for Chocolate", Common, 2000

"Miss E... So Addictive", Missy Elliott, 2001

"Sound-Dust", Stereolab, 2001

"Original Pirate Material", The Streets, 2002

"All Hail West Texas", The Mountain Goats, 2002

"Dead Cities, Red Seas & Lost Ghosts", M83, 2003

"Sonic Nurse", Sonic Youth, 2004

"End of the World Party (Just in Case)", Medeski Martin & Wood, 2004

"Anniemal", Annie, 2004

"Rejoicing in the Hands of the Golden Empress", Devendra Banhart, 2004

"The Early Years", The Early Years, 2006

"Drum's Not Dead", Liars, 2006

"Everything All the Time", Band of Horses, 2006

"The Cool", Lupe Fiasco, 2007

"Un Día", Juana Molina, 2008

"The Way I See It", Raphael Saadiq, 2008

"Antidotes", Foals, 2008

"The Ecstatic", Mos Def, 2009

"Love Comes Close", Cold Cave, 2009

"Embryonic", The Flaming Lips, 2009

"Cosmogramma", Flying Lotus, 2010

"Queen of Denmark", John Grant, 2010

"Smother", Wild Beasts, 2011

"Anna Calvi", Anna Calvi, 2011

"Outside", O'Death, 2011

"Heaven", The Walkmen, 2012

"The Haunted Man", Bat for Lashes, 2012

"The Idler Wheel Is Wiser Than the Driver of the Screw and Whipping Cords Will Serve You More Than Ropes Will Ever Do", Fiona Apple, 2012

"Wondrous Bughouse", Youth Lagoon, 2013

"Small Town Heroes", Hurray for the Riff Raff, 2014

"Wine Dark Sea", Jolie Holland, 2014

"1989", Taylor Swift, 2014

"Blank Project", Neneh Cherry, 2014

"B'lieve I'm Goin' Down", Kurt Vile, 2015

"Apocalypse, Girl", Jenny Hval, 2015

"Fading Frontier", Deerhunter, 2015

"Midwest Farmer's Daughter", Margo Price, 2016

"Changes", Charles Bradley, 2016

"Run the Jewels 3", Run the Jewels, 2016

"Sketches of Brunswick East", King Gizzard and the Lizard Wizard, 2017

"Rocket", (Sandy) Alex G, 2017

ACKNOWLEDGEMENTS

• • • • •

I'd like to thank several people who influenced my love for music and, in turn, this book. I'll start with my mother, Mary O'Connor, who introduced me to The Beatles. Mom, your bird can't sing, but he finally got this project to come together.

Eric Schroeck, you influenced about half by CD purchases in the nineties, then stuck around to get me into Stevie Wonder and Sufjan Stevens.

Pat Moynihan, you turned me on to classic rock, then provided half of my 2000s music education, and were still there to introduce me to Wye Oak. Without you, I'd be starless and bible black.

Ryan Marston, you filled in the other half of my 2000s education, keeping my tastes young when I started wearing dad jeans. I would've eventually discovered The National anyway, but as always, you were there before they were cool.

Jaron Shevy, you never let music or life be anything less than great fun and taught me that there's nothing wrong with loving Blur and Oasis at the same time.

Mark Losinger, in addition to the editing support, thank you for playing "Let It Bleed" in the dark at Grammy's. Oh, and for expanding my jazz collection and my hip-hop collection, distracting me with decades of R&B singles from lackluster albums, and giving me the free hit of Pavement that got me hooked.

Tamara Jones, thank you for the invaluable graphic design support. This book was U2 in my own hands, but it's Radiohead in yours.

Further thanks to Grace Peirce of Great Life Press and Dianne Fazio at Walch Education and Printing.

To the community at besteveralbums.com, thank you for your ratings, your reviews, and the hint that there are people like me out there who might actually read this book someday.

And last but not least, to my wife, Jill, and my kids, Jocelyn and Calvin: Thank you for sharing this hobby with me these last 50,000-or-so waking hours... and for introducing me to Bruce, Ani, and Ray.

INDEX

• • • • •

BRYAN O'CONNOR

Bryan O'Connor is a nonprofit accountant by day, an author of puns on baseball players' names by night, and a compulsive consumer of popular (and less popular) music whenever he's awake. He once taught himself the flute solo from "California Dreamin'" on the recorder, but has no other music credits to his name. He lives in Cumberland, Maine, which has no concert venues, recordstores, or, presumably, other people who like Charles Mingus.

Made in the USA
San Bernardino, CA
23 February 2020

64853177R00084